# A PRODUCER'S
# BROADWAY JOURNEY

# A PRODUCER'S BROADWAY JOURNEY

*~*

## Stuart Ostrow

Westport, Connecticut
London

**Library of Congress Cataloging-in-Publication Data**

Ostrow, Stuart, 1932–
    A producer's Broadway journey / Stuart Ostrow.
      p.   cm.
    Includes bibliographical references and index.
    ISBN 0–275–95866–3 (alk. paper)
    1. Musicals—New York (State)—New York—History and criticism.
    2. Broadway (New York, N.Y.)—History.   I. Title.
ML1711.8.N3O88   1999
782.1'4'097471—dc21       97–46533
                 MN

British Library Cataloguing in Publication Data is available.

Library of Congress Catalog Card Number: 97–46533
ISBN: 0–275–95866–3

First published in 1999

Praeger Publishers, 88 Post Road West, Westport, CT 06881
An imprint of Greenwood Publishing Group, Inc.
www.praeger.com

Printed in the United States of America

The paper used in this book complies with the
Permanent Paper Standard issued by the National
Information Standards Organization (Z39.48–1984).

10 9 8 7 6 5 4 3 2 1

*To my students at the University of Houston School of Theatre, and to my wife, Ann, who continues to make the journey meaningful.*

# Contents

# Contents

## Part V: 1990–1998—
### *Stomp, Rent, Bring in 'Da Noise Bring in 'Da Funk:*
### Quo Vadis?

*Photographs follow page 76*

# Preface

The basis for this book was a seminar at the University of Houston School of Theatre entitled "The Broadway Musical Canon: Mid-Century to the Millennium." It was a joy to teach and happily elicited this comment from one student: "I feel I should be taking this class with a martini in my hand." Exactly. I intended it to be both a celebration of the Broadway musical and a meditation on what has caused its decline. My students' enthusiasm and eagerness to learn about the esoteric nature of the musical reminded me that other than jazz, the musical is the only indigenous American art form and precious little has been written cogently about it by a practitioner. Since there are dozens of critical theatre collections written by lofty academics, I decided to write an informal standard of judgment according to my thirty-eight years of professional experience, and call it A *Producer's Broadway Journey*.

These particular sixty-three shows, covering five decades and approximately five hundred musicals, doubtless reflect some accidents of my personal taste; nevertheless they, arguably, represent the best of the last forty-nine years of the Broadway Musical theatre. There are personal references and anecdotes; some are tragic, some comic, or merely human, and they are included as evidence of my journey, and in an effort to illuminate the characters and ambitions of those I met along the way. It is also a subjective evaluation of those tangible and intangible essentials that make a musical fly, or keep it earthbound.

# Introduction

I want you to know as you read this precisely who I am and what is on my mind. I want you to understand exactly who you are getting: You are getting a man who for some time now has felt radically separated from most of the ideas that seem to interest the Mafiosi of success and failure of the Great White Way. The forces suppressing quality musical theatre today are the Broadway establishment, which prefers to buy the future rather than undertake the labor of making it, and the conservative constituency in the National Endowment for the Arts (NEA), who insist musical theatre is not high culture and therefore should be relegated to a lower level of federal recognition and financial support. It is vital to do battle against both, for they are grievously in error.

Let's start with the Feds. The danger in the air, originated by the arts-conservatives, is to the effect that the NEA should divorce the shotgun administration of opera and musical theatre and return opera to the Music Program whence it came and where it belongs. These appointees to the National Council of the Arts consider themselves the guardians of opera's treasury and imply its coupling with musical theatre is akin to a mixed marriage, where the chances of a lasting union are doomed and its progeny is to be cursed. Because I am a musician, produce new Broadway musicals, am a founding panel member of the NEA's opera-musical program, and have been happily mixed-married to the same woman for forty-two years, I feel qualified to attempt to neutralize their intellectual prejudice.

Why can't we live together? Will *Porgy and Bess, Candide, Sweeney Todd,* or *Einstein on the Beach* diminish an opera audience's passion for *Fidelio* or *Montezuma?* Hardly. What upsets the preservers of the past most about our consanguinity is the fear that we will produce hybrid, inferior musical works instead of "treasures of civilization" (past operatic master-pieces), and will continue to neglect the genius of our own twentieth-century composers: Douglas Moore, Virgil Thompson, Samuel Barber, Howard Hanson, Roger Sessions, Carlisle Floyd, and Aaron Copland. They speak clearly about the lack of lasting American art since the end of World War II, but are disingenuous when suggesting that it has some-thing to do with breeding; they ridicule the possibility that opera and musical theatre artists could discover creative common ground. The truth is their interest in the musical is limited, and their opinion of Broadway is that it represents at best an uneasy marriage between musicians of generally serious background and the lure of show-business fame. Opera remains an elite form, European and in some sense romantic in origin, belonging in large measure to the domain of high culture and recalling the past rather than mirroring contemporary daily life. There is no room, in their opinion, for Gershwin, Rodgers, Sondheim, Porter, Bernstein, Kern, Berlin, Loesser, or Weill. No room for the indigenous American art form, yesterday or today.

There's much that's quixotic about Federal funding for the arts; I agree with John Updike when he says, "I would rather have as my patron a host of anonymous citizens digging into their own pockets for the price of a book or a magazine than a small body of enlightened and responsible men and women administering public funds."

This topic next brings me to the Broadway bureaucracy. I have mixed emotions about having created the *Pippin* commercial that I put on tele-vision in 1973. The commercial was the first of its kind, a minute of lightning in a bottle, but it never occurred to me that it would change the way theatre was to be produced. From that moment on hucksters could sell shows as commodities so long as their spot had glitter and hype. Never mind producing a great show, produce a great commercial! Every-one became a theatre impresario overnight—lawyers, landlords, invest-ment bankers, motion picture moguls, dilettantes, and a precious few genuinely talented young producers.

In 1961, when I was trying out my first solo-producer musical, *We Take the Town*, starring Robert Preston as Pancho Villa at the Shubert Theatre in Philadelphia, Mel Brooks was the bookwriter for another new musi-cal, *All American*, starring Ray Bolger and directed by Joshua Logan at the Erlanger Theatre down the block. Both shows were in deep trouble and Mel and I commiserated. Brooks would scream about how crazy Lo-gan was. He said that every time they tried to fix a number, instead of rehearsing, Logan had the producers bring a five-course meal from

Bookbinders restaurant to the theatre, and they all had to watch him eat! Brooks wasn't a writer anymore—he was a *waiter*. Perhaps you can understand why seven years later Mel wrote and directed his classic film-spoof, *The Producers*, and never wrote anything else for the stage. I nevertheless have spent the past thirty-eight years producing on Broadway and am here today not to praise Brooks, but to bury him.

Oscar Hammerstein II, remembering Theresa Helburn of the Theatre Guild, put it this way: "I think only people in the theatre know what a producer is. The public does not know. It knows a writer writes, and an actor acts, and a director tells them what to do. A producer raises money. Well, he does, and in some cases that's all he does. But the workers in the theatre know that this is not the real thing. A producer is a rare, paradoxical genius—hard-headed, soft-hearted, cautious, reckless, a hopeful innocent in fair weather, a stern pilot in stormy weather, a mathematician who prefers to ignore the laws of mathematics and trust intuition, an idealist, a realist, a practical dreamer, a sophisticated gambler, a stage-struck child. That's a producer." Thirty-eight years ago, promising himself not to keep his dreams within reason was a reasonable credo for an aspiring young producer. Today it is the exception. Today the theatre is ruled by bottom-line thinking. Who's the star? What does it cost? When will it recoup? Where is the profit-earnings ratio? How will it play in Nutley and Nagasaki?

When I started out as Frank Loesser's apprentice, he told me in no uncertain terms: "A producer is someone who knows a writer—loud is good—and work in the theatre because you'll always have someplace to go after dinner." Frank also taught me how to define quality: "The best skill and effort possible to produce the finest and most admirable result possible." Armed with these commandments, I began my Broadway journey.

Creativity always came as a surprise to me; therefore, I could never count on it and dared not believe in it until it had happened. To deal with uncertainty I had enough faith in the future to take risks—a musical about the signing of the Declaration of Independence, a drama concerning a Chinese transvestite communist spy and a French diplomat, a comedy of manners in rhymed couplets, and an unlikely musical set in Charlemagne's Holy Roman Empire. Faith makes the earth move, evokes commitments; risk propels adventure and innovation. A theatre ruled by faith and risk rather than rational calculus will call forth an endless stream of invention and art. Agnes De Mille insisted, "Living is a form of not being sure, not knowing what next or how. The moment you know you begin to die a little. The artist never entirely knows. We guess. We may be wrong but we take leap after leap in the dark."

In these meretricious times when many incipient theatrical talents seek refuge in Hollywood or quit altogether, looking for new writers, plays, and musicals and producing them is the best solution for keeping the fabulous invalid alive. The nonprofit theatre is not the answer. Their struggle for subsidies and grants limits the gamble they will take on new works, especially musicals and expensive plays, and recently there are signs that the government will require the right of censorship before administering any funds. The individual entrepreneur, the lone gun, the stubborn independent, has always been our best hope. Sam Harris, Leland Hayward, David Merrick, Richard Barr, Hal Prince, Binkie Beaumont, Michael Codron, and Cameron Mackintosh are a few that come to mind. Successful new producers will attract unconventional capital investment, thereby reducing the landlord's influence in the theatre, and will possibly stem the cultural malaise that began with their reign twenty-seven years ago. Sensing the lack of producers in the seventies, directors, authors, and actors produced their own work, and with too few exceptions, failed. Not until the balance between theatre owners and producers is restored (the so-called League of American Theatres and Producers is a front for theatre owners) and the thrust of production is to create new works will we have a vibrant, healthy commercial theatre.

Finally, what can be said about the place we need to be? We need a new salon where unique works are produced, where writers can compare, debate, and challenge the pain and passion of creating original musicals, operas, and perhaps yet undiscovered theatrical forms. Why not create a cradle, a place of origin and continuity where first-time dramatists and song writers are nurtured, and whose original works are ultimately produced on and beyond Broadway? We need to teach the student writer to dramatize action, inspire the incipient novelist, poet, and journalist to create insight and humor through lyrics and librettos, and encourage the new composers of MTV, opera, and minimalist music to fuse with the art of telling stories. If enough marriages can be nurtured between these crossover worlds, we will begin to illuminate the human condition for a vast audience. It might even produce some stagestruck children who would grow up to ignore the bottom line and risk everything. There was a time on Broadway when theatre was a shot fired around the world, and it would change your life, and it happened at least once every season, and once was enough. So I begin this book with three of the most hopeful words in the English language. To be continued.

# PART I
## 1950–1960

# Broadway Babies: Adler and Ross, Stephen Sondheim, Bock and Harnick, and Meredith Willson

In the fifties the parameters of the American musical theatre were five blocks long by about one and a half blocks wide; from Forty-fourth to Forty-ninth Streets, between Eighth Avenue and Broadway. Dinty Moore's and Sardi's restaurants were the club hangouts and the League of New York Theatres was a loose confederation of enlightened, talented, risk-taking Broadway producers: Feuer and Martin, Leland Hayward, Cheryl Crawford, Robert Fryer, Griffith and Prince, Herman Levin, Kermit Bloomgarden, David Merrick, and a few passive theatre landlords who periodically negotiated collective bargaining agreements with the actors', musicians', and stagehands' unions. It was an exciting cottage industry with lots of old-fashioned kickbacks, extortion, and patronage for those who played the management-labor game. The average musical cost $150,000 to produce and the price of a ticket was $7. There were as many as ninety attractions electric-lighted on Broadway in one season and it was not uncommon for sixteen of them to be musicals. The New York middle-class audience went to the theatre at least five times a year—new productions were prolific, and hit songs from Broadway musicals were heard everywhere. The reign of Irving Berlin, Cole Porter, and Rodgers and Hammerstein was nearly over. Loesser, Lerner and Loewe, Bernstein, Comden and Green, and Jule Styne, all of whom started in the late forties, were at the peak of their creativity with *Guys and Dolls*, *Wonderful Town*, *My Fair Lady*, and *Gypsy*, but it was the new kids on the block who would set the pace for the next generation. Dick Adler and Jerry Ross wrote *The Pajama Game* and *Damn Yankees*, back to back hits; twenty-seven-year-old lyricist Stephen Sondheim's collaboration with Leonard Bernstein and Jule Styne was auspicious; Jerry Bock's and Sheldon Harnick's *Fiorello!* won the Pulitzer Prize; and Meredith Willson marched into town with *The Music Man.*

There were dozens of young producers trying their wings in the fifties, which is one reason why the theatre soared. I made my way into the legitimate theatre at twenty-two, working for Frank Loesser, and have been a stage-struck child since. Since I was a trained musician (clarinetist) in search of a career, my music education brought me closer to understanding the composer's goals and realizing my own aspirations to be creative. Writers trusted my instincts and I was continually shooting arrows into the air, hoping that they might fall somewhere that counted. If you can't write, produce. For the moment, however, I had to be content helping to find, publish, and plug hit songs for Frank Music Corp.: "Unchained Melody," "Cry Me a River," "The Twelfth of Never," and "Yellowbird" made me a contender.

Yip Harburg said, "Music makes you feel a feeling, words make you think a thought. A song makes you feel a thought." And it takes a creative producer to present it to the public, I said to myself. So, obeying Loesser's first commandment, I began cultivating new and experienced theatre writers: Norman Gimbel, Hugh Martin and Ralph Blaine, Ogden Nash and Vernon Duke, Oscar Brown, Jr., Lew Spence, Marilyn and Alan Bergman, Arthur Hamilton, Jerry Livingston and Paul Francis Webster, Alex North, Rod McKuen, Jay Livingston and Ray Evans, Hoagy Carmichael, Sammy Cahn and James Van Heusen, Mark McIntyre, Bob Wells, Sammy Fain, David Amram, Milton Schafer, Lee Pockriss and Hal David, Peter Udell, Robert Waldman and Alfred Uhry, Hy Zaret and Lou Singer, Charles Gaynor, Phil Springer, Ervin Drake, Julie Mandel, Fran Landesman and Tommy Wolf, Richard Lewine and Arnold Horwitt, Richard Maltby and David Shire, Billy Goldenberg, Bob James and Jack O'Brien, and Helen Deutsch.

When the new decade began I flew to London to tell Frank I had to leave to produce my first solo musical. He was annoyed but smiled and said, "What the hell, I've had the best years of your life, and don't forget, producers come and go; copyrights are forever." He was right of course, so when in 1994 the late William Henry III, *Time* magazine drama critic, called me an endangered species, I thought it was the saddest compliment I'd ever earned.

# 1950–1951

Forty-Sixth Street Theatre
Opened Friday, November 24, 1950
Feuer and Martin present:

## Guys and Dolls

Based on a Story and Characters by Damon Runyon; Music and Lyrics by Frank Loesser; Book by Jo Swerling and Abe Burrows; Dances and Musical Numbers staged by Michael Kidd; Settings and Lighting by Jo Mielziner; Costumes by Alvin Colt; Staged by George S. Kaufman. *Cast*: Sam Levine, Vivian Blaine, Robert Alda.

My Broadway journey began with Frank Loesser. I was a student in Manhattan's High School of Music & Art and my first big date was with a knockout cello player who was also a devotee of Broadway musicals. She bought two balcony seats to *Guys and Dolls* for my birthday and we sat mesmerized watching and listening to a trio of horse-players sing "Fugue for Tinhorns," then a Salvation Army chorale imploring gamblers to "Follow the Fold," and a flood of surprising, funny songs—canons and gospels—sexy, gymnastic dances, thrilling orchestration and vocal arrangements, and a new language, where Hotbox strippers tell their boy friends to take back their "poils," because they're not one of those "goils." At the final curtain I was hopelessly in love. Not so much with the knockout cello player as with the Broadway musical. And when I was a twenty-one-year-old buck sergeant in the United States Air Force in 1953, producer/director of various camp shows and weekly network radio broadcasts during our Korean Police Action, my love affair with *Guys and Dolls* paid off.

The Air Force wanted a morale building National Touring Stage Show along the lines of Irving Berlin's *This Is the Army* and Moss Hart's *Winged Victory* to commemorate the fiftieth anniversary of powered flight, and they asked me to produce it. I convinced the Colonel in charge that professional writers were needed (Frank Loesser, of course) and hitched a C-54 ride to Mitchell Air Force Base in Long Island. I gave the elevator man at Manhattan's Warwick Hotel twenty bucks to tell me what floor Mr. Loesser was on, and rang the doorbell in the tower suite. It was a payoff that changed my life. Looking like a small dapper Anthony Quinn, and as warm and funny and smart as anyone I have ever known, Frank Loesser invited me in and we drank up the night. We exchanged loop-to-loop concepts for the Air Force musical and I swear he even wrote a lyric for a General who gambled: "Old crap-shooters never die, they just stay faded," he ad-libbed at the piano. After a couple of deals before dawn, Frank announced he would write the score, only if I hired Abe Burrows to write the book. Was I dreaming? I had lunch the next day with Burrows at the 21 Club, and was back in Washington, D.C., that afternoon with an agreement from two Broadway giants—the creators of my *Guys and Dolls*, to write the USAF *Conquest of the Air*. The colonel thought I was a genius and gave me a three-day pass. The following week I was told to appear before the Senate Government Operations Committee's Permanent Subcommittee on Investigations. I was asked what my political affiliations were, was I ever a member of the Labor Party, wasn't my father born in Kiev, Russia? It was frightening. What did this have to do with putting on a show for the Air Force? It wasn't until my Colonel vouched for me and explained that McCarthyism was in the air—synonymous with political opportunism and public character assassination—and that Abe Burrows was under investigation for alleged Communist sympathy, that I realized what Loesser's intention was. If the United States Air Force would hire Burrows, the witch hunt would stop. It was why Frank agreed to write the musical, giving up a year of his life and putting his reputation on the line. It was called friendship. In the end my chicken Colonel wouldn't fight the barnyard cocks and I had to tell Frank Loesser and Abe Burrows the Air Force couldn't use them.

After my release from the service, Loesser's Frank Music Corp. hired me and I worked my way up the ladder from song plugger to press agent to governor general of the Hollywood office to vice president and General Professional Manager at twenty-eight. It was seven years good luck and I like to think there was enough of J. Pierrepoint Finch in me to have earned Frank's farewell letter when I quit to produce my first Broadway musical. It arrived with a $10,000 check, a lot of money in 1961—the year *How To Succeed in Business Without Really Trying* opened—which simply, but to me grandeloquently, said: "I believe in you. Love, Frank."

Frank was all about taking chances. Never allowing himself to become too comfortable with subject, tone, rhythm, or syntax. Unlike Alan Jay Lerner, who, after *My Fair Lady* and *Gigi*, said he had found his sound. Loesser leaped from English farce, *Where's Charley?*, to Manhattan mugs, *Guys and Dolls*, to Napa Valley sweethearts, *The Most Happy Fella*. His genius for writing authentic lyrics and muscular music set the tone of *Guys and Dolls* by having its Broadway denizens sing in Runyonesque patois, as in this example from the title song sung by two main stem gamblers reciting odds: "Call it sad / Call it funny / But it's better than even money / Call it hell / Call it heaven / It's a probable twelve to seven." In the first four bars of "Fugue For Tinhorns," Loesser not only confirms half the title of the show by having Nicely Nicely Johnson reading and singing from a racing form: "And here's a *guy* that says if the weather's clear / Can do," but also establishes the character's métier. Bennie Southstreet adds more bookie lingo: "I'm picking Valentine 'cause on the morning line / The guy has got him figured at five to nine / Has chance," and finally Rusty Charlie verifies the show's New York City locale by citing one of its 1950 daily newspapers: "But look at Epitaph, he wins it by a half / According to this here in the *Telegraph*." For this fugue Loesser composed a more complicated canon than "Frere Jaques" but the musical satisfaction of listening to three separate stories with the same overlapping melody was just as enjoyable. Phrases such as "feed box noise," "no bum steer," and "a handicapper that's real sincere" came straight from the horse's mouth and transported us into fable.

*Guys and Dolls* director George S. Kaufman was the celebrated author of *Once in a Lifetime, You Can't Take It With You*, and *The Man Who Came To Dinner*. A member of the legendary Algonquin Round Table, Kaufman was known for the destructive wisecrack, the verbal ricochet, and it was never more resonant than when fledgling bookwriter Abe Burrows proudly boasted "Fugue For Tinhorns" would take place on a treadmill, a stunt never before performed by actors on Broadway. "Isn't that great, George?" asked Abe, breathlessly. Deadpan, Kaufman replied: "That depends upon what they are saying on the treadmill, Mr. Burrows."

Burrows never asked Kaufman another question. Another tense moment was addressed when Kaufman, Loesser, and producer Cy Feuer took a taxicab to New Jersey in order to see Mielziner's set being built. The cabby zoomed through downtown onto the West Side Highway, running three red lights and nearly mowing down an old lady. The passengers were silent with fear and not a word had been spoken until the George Washington Bridge came into sight. At that moment, taciturn Kaufman gently tapped the crazed driver on the shoulder: "See that bridge, driver?" asked Kaufman. "Yea, so what?" the driver sneered. Kaufman leaned over and whispered into his ear: "Don't cross it until you come to it."

"Follow the Fold" starts off as a typical Salvation Army hymn: "Follow the fold and stray no more / Put down the bottle and we'll say no more," Sister Sarah and her group pray. Then an unexpected afterthought—an extra pick-up bar leading back to the chorus: "Before you take another swallow" makes us laugh. In another parody, "The Oldest Established," guys sing of the Biltmore garage wanting a grand and not having a grand on hand, being a good scout, looking for action even when the heat is on; then joining in pious harmony to sing an oxymoron: "To the oldest established permanent floating crap game in New York." In "Adelaide's Lament" the character gets her tips from a medical journal rather than a racing form, and diagnoses her cold symptoms as being caused by too many postponed wedding dates. It remains a classic comic turn for broads with a Bronx accent. "My Time of Day" is a soliloquy in which we're given a glimpse into the character's soul; in this case, a surprisingly poetic one hidden within a mug's demeanor. Sky Masterson is the most adventurous gambler on the street; he has won his bet that he could get prim and proper Salvation Army Sarah to Havana to spend the night with him. Now that she's had too much to drink, for the clincher, he sings: "When the smell of the rain-washed pavement / Comes up clean and fresh and cold / And the street lamp light fills the gutter with gold / That's my time of day / And you're the only doll I've ever wanted to share it with me." It also gave Loesser another chance to compose a beautiful melody with difficult intervals, ninths, as he did before with the popular standard, "Spring Will Be a Little Late This Year." "More I Cannot Wish You," the show's charm song, was given to beloved vaudevillian Pat Rooney, Sr., who plays fairy Godfather to Sarah, and wishes her a lover: "With the sheep's eye / And the lickerish tooth."

One final untold story regarding *Guys and Dolls*, this one about the movie version. Hollywood adaptations of hit Broadway musicals, with too few exceptions, fail. Why? For openers, you don't photograph sweat, the crucial result of energy on stage. Whereas it is the theatre's aim to transform commentary into dramatic action, films indulge in reaction shots and romantic close-ups. Stage scenery is an abstraction, movies love panoramic reality. The most difficult transition to overcome, however, is the movie star. Samuel Goldwyn's movie of *Guys and Dolls* was no exception and brought Frank head to head with another Frank—Sinatra—who insisted on crooning Nathan Detroit's half-spoken begrudging apology to Adelaide for postponing yet another wedding date: "Alright already! / I'm just a no good-nick / Alright already it's true, so nu? / So sue me." When Loesser heard the throbbing string section accompany Sinatra at the pre-recording session, he belted him, right in front of Goldwyn and director Joe Mankiewicz, and was banned from the set. Which is why Marlon Brando, who was playing Sky Masterson, wound up with the new hit song, "A Woman In Love," originally intended for Sinatra.

---

Imperial Theatre
Opened Thursday, October 12, 1950
Leland Hayward presents:

# Call Me Madam

Music and Lyrics by Irving Berlin; Book by Howard Lindsay and Russel Crouse; Directed by George Abbott; Dances and Musical Numbers staged by Jerome Robbins; Scenery and Costumes by Raoul Pene du Bois.
*Cast:* Ethel Merman, Russell Nype, Paul Lucas.

Irving Berlin *is* American songwriting and although his Broadway output was not as prolific as Rodgers & Hammerstein's or Cole Porter's, his genius for matching emotion with melody and lyric was unequaled. His songs were simple and direct and often old-fashioned because he wanted you to feel you could have written them. (Berlin loved the phrase "old fashioned"; indeed, he used it in *Miss Liberty* for "Let's Take an Old Fashioned Walk," and again in *Call Me Madam*, reminding us "Marrying for Love" is an old-fashioned idea.) Listen to "Always," and the inevitability of its title: "I'll be loving you / Always, with a love that's true / Always / . . . Not for just an hour / Not for just a day / Not for just a year / But always." Or his musical emphasis on the "won-" of wonderful from "They Say It's Wonderful": "They say that falling in love is wonderful / It's wonderful / So they say."

The great Irving Berlin was 62 when he wrote *Call Me Madam*, a parody of Washington's famous party-giver-appointed-Ambassador to Luxembourg Pearl Mesta. He gave the character (as played by Ethel Merman) a terrific verse to "The Hostess with the Mostes' on the Ball," but the show was not in the same class as his past Broadway hits: *Ziegfeld Follies*, *As Thousands Cheer*, *Louisiana Purchase*, *This Is the Army*, and *Annie Get Your Gun*. As for *Call Me Madam*, Merman was the powerhouse. You could hear every lyric, no matter how difficult the melody, and she never missed a performance. The intrepid theatregoer could count on her, snow, rain, gloom of night, and lack of microphones notwithstanding. The duet she sang with Russell Nype, "You're Just in Love," seemed too close for comfort to Loesser's 1949 "Baby It's Cold Outside," for me, until Frank told me that Berlin had invented the contrapuntal pop song in 1914 with "Play a Simple Melody" and that he was imitating the master. La Merman and "It's a Lovely Day Today," "Marrying for Love," and "The Best Thing for You Would Be Me" made *Madam* Berlin's last hit Broadway musical.

Many trunk songs have found their way in and out of Broadway musicals; for example, Frank Loesser's "A Bushel and a Peck" from *Guys and Dolls* was originally written for a Betty Hutton movie, and Cole Porter's "From This Moment On" was dropped from *Out of This World*, only to wind up in the film version of *Kiss Me Kate*. Berlin was no exception. For *As Thousands Cheer*, he went into his trunk and found "Smile and Show Your Dimple," which he changed to "Easter Parade." Piece of cake. If you're Irving.

---

St. James Theatre
Opened Thursday, March 29, 1951
Rodgers and Hammerstein present:

# The King and I

Music by Richard Rodgers; Book and Lyrics by Oscar Hammerstein II; Based on the Novel *Anna and the King of Siam* by Margaret Landen; Directed by Jon van Druten; Settings and Lighting by Jo Mielziner; Costumes Designed by Irene Sharaff; Choreography by Jerome Robbins. *Cast*: Gertrude Lawrence, Yul Brynner, Doretta Morrow.

At mid-century Rogers & Hammerstein were the crowned heads of Broadway, having reinvented the musical form with *Oklahoma!*, *Carousel*, *South Pacific*, and now *The King and I*. They were the class act on the block, and as if they needed to prove it, adapted the novel *Anna and the King of Siam* for the very British star Gertrude Lawrence. Although *The King and I* was set on the other side of the world—exotic Siam—with a despotic King being taught the ways of the West by a cultured British governess, opposites were attracted to each other, just like Sarah and Sky. "Hello, Young Lovers" had the difficult assignment of convincing audiences that a middle-aged widow could feel romance. It succeeded due to an exquisite lyric and a charming melody for a leading lady with a limited vocal range. Both Lawrence and Yul Brynner were superb actors, but not great voices, and so began the era of speak-singing. (Lerner and Loewe capitalized on the style seven years later for another Brit, Rex Harrison, in *My Fair Lady*.) Spoken or sung, the score was wonderful. The charming Gertrude, in her best Noël Coward delivery, delivered: "Whenever I feel afraid / I hold my head erect / And whistle a happy tune." Note the similarity to another Hammerstein lyric: "When you walk through a storm / Hold your head up high." Hammerstein's eternal optimism was matched by Rodgers' buoyant melody. (R&H were masters of the art: "You'll Never Walk Alone," "Climb Ev'ry Mountain," and "You've Got to Be Carefully Taught.")

Even Buddha couldn't show the way to a confused monarch in "A

Puzzlement," compelling King Yul to shout; so the big ballads were given to supporting characters with trained voices. Opera's Dorothy Sarnoff, as Lady Thiang, one of the King's many wives, informs us her lord and master is a man who thinks with his heart, stumbles and falls, yet tries again, and now and then says, "Something Wonderful." It was an unusual soliloquy sung by one character about another. Soprano Doretta Morrow and tenor Larry Douglas caressed the high notes in "We Kiss in a Shadow," but the show-stoppers were written for and performed by Gertrude Lawrence; and wow, did she know how to thrill an audience! One of the most memorable moments in Broadway history was when Anna teaches the King how to, in "Shall We Dance?" (The three after-beats in the tune were used by Jerome Robbins to emphasize the arduous necessity of keeping in step—and ultimately as a demonstration of their ability to fly!) "Getting to Know You" was the other; when upper-class English Anna puts it her way, but nicely: "You are precisely / My cup of tea."

When Gertrude Lawrence died of cancer during the run, replacing her was a monumental problem until casting director John Fearnley suggested a brilliant actress from the Yiddish Theatre on Second Avenue—Miriam Silverstein, the Streisand of her day. Rodgers was intrigued but Hammerstein doubted she could lose her Jewish accent. Nevertheless they rehearsed day and night, and miraculously the actress was able to perfect a British enunciation worthy of royalty. Her audition astonished everyone when, in flawless English, she sang: "Getting to know you / Getting to know all about you." An incredulous Hammerstein turned to Fearnley: "You're a genius, John," he complimented. A moment later, Silverstein concluded with "You are precisely / My *glass* of tea."

---

Alvin Theatre
Opened Thursday, April 19, 1951
George Abbott in association with Robert Fryer presents:

# A Tree Grows in Brooklyn

Book by Betty Smith and George Abbott; Based on Miss Smith's novel of the same name; Music by Arthur Schwartz; Lyrics by Dorothy Fields;

Scenery and Costumes by Irene Scharaff; Choreography by Herbert
Ross; Directed by George Abbott.
*Cast:* Shirley Booth, Johnny Johnston, Marcia Van Dyke.

It was *A Tree Grows in Brooklyn*'s misfortune to open in the same season
as *Guys and Dolls, The King and I*, and *Call Me Madam*, and as a result it
was never rightly acclaimed. Arthur Schwartz and Dorothy Fields wrote
an enchanting score featuring yet another great actress/speak-singer, Shirley Booth, and a terrific new leading man, pop singer Johnny Johnston.
Johnston, playing a struggling alcoholic, owned "I'm Like a New Broom"
and the touching "I'll Buy You a Star": "Not just a star but the best one
in the sky / But I won't rest until I buy the moon." Fields knew how to
make us care for her characters, and melodies poured out of Schwartz—
none lovelier than "Make the Man Love Me." The music staff was the
best in the business: Jay Blackton, Joe Glover, Robert Russell Bennett,
and Max Goberman, and Mr. Abbott introduced another brilliant choreographer to Broadway, Herbert Ross. (In addition to Jerome Robbins,
Abbott also gave Bob Fosse his first gig.) Recent attempts to revive *A
Tree Grows in Brooklyn* have been foiled by the creators' estates, which
correctly insist on not sharing any subsidiary rights with the Society of
Stage Directors and Choreographers.

## OTHER MUSICALS

*Michael Todd's Peep Show* opened the 1950–1951 Broadway season with
songs by Sammy Fain, Harold Rome, and Jule Styne. Gian-Carlo Menotti
premiered *The Telephone* and *The Medium*, as did Benjamin Britten with
*Let's Make an Opera*. Cole Porter's songs "Use Your Imagination" and
"Nobody's Chasing Me" were squandered in Agnes de Mille's production
of *Out of This World*. All in all, an unparalleled season, not to be repeated
in the next five decades.

# 1951–1952

Sam S. Shubert Theatre
Opened Monday, November 12, 1951
Cheryl Crawford presents:

## Paint Your Wagon

Book and Lyrics by Alan Jay Lerner; Music by Frederick Loewe; Dances
and Musical Ensembles by Agnes De Mille; Scenery designed by Oliver
Smith; Costumes designed by Motley; Lighting by Peggy Clark; Directed
by Daniel Mann.
*Cast*: James Barton, Olga San Juan, James Mitchell, Tony Bavaar.

*Paint Your Wagon* was Lerner and Loewe's second Broadway musical
following their hit *Brigadoon*; in it, Viennese operetta composer Loewe
and New York department-store-heir-turned-lyricist Lerner brilliantly
evoked a mythical Scottish valley. Believing a European composer could
make a 1853 California mining town sing was a leap of faith for musical
theatre audiences, but Loewe didn't let them down. "I Talk to the Trees,"
"They Call the Wind Maria," "I Still See Elisa," and "Wand'rin' Star"
were authentic, haunting reflections of the early West. Obviously, great
music doesn't have an accent.
   "They Call the Wind Maria" blew the stars around Oliver Smith's
cloud-filled cyclorama sky and made "the mountains sound / Like folks
were up there dyin'." It was a wailing, whining, rushing wind of a melody,

and Lerner's lyric for "Wand'rin' Star" was the forerunner of Frank Loesser's "Joey, Joey, Joey" from *The Most Happy Fella*. In their soliloquy song, "I Talk To the Trees," Loewe's accompaniment strums Spanish guitars while Lerner has Julio reveal his innermost wishes to a señorita: "I tell you my dreams / And while you're listening to me / I suddenly see them come true." Then a charming beguine coda, as Julio imagines an April night, sipping brandy, reading poetry, and asking for a dance. Lyric poetry and great musical theatre. In "I Still See Elisa," Lerner is not shy about feeling masculine (an emotion seldom expressed by lyricists today) when a father tells his daughter how much he loved her dead mother: "I still hear Elisa / And still have a yearning / To hold her against me again." It's no wonder Alan Jay Lerner married eight times; he loved women.

The production boasted yet another legendary Broadway music department: Franz Allers, Ted Royal, and Trude Rittman, all of whom enhanced Loewe's music by adding orchestration, vocals, and dance arrangements. (Don Walker's orchestrations for *The Most Happy Fella* are as much part of Loesser's score as the composer's lyrics.) With few exceptions, auxiliary Broadway music is written by others. The best (and least publicized) composers-for-hire are dance arrangers. After rehearsing for weeks, Trude Rittman will have taken Agnes de Mille's rhythmic dictation, which is a breakdown of how many bars of music are needed to execute a dance combination, step, or pas de deux, including the musical accents and the dynamics the choreographer feels are necessary to express the dancer's character, joy, and fear. Composing "dummy music" to blueprint the creation of the ballet/dance, Rittman must then recompose it entirely using Loewe's melodies.

It was a lackluster season for musicals, so here is an anecdote Alan Lerner told me regarding 1947's *Brigadoon* and the famous sword dance. Agnes De Mille insisted dancer James Mitchell be accompanied by two authentic bagpipes players. It was difficult enough finding one, let alone two, bagpipers in New York, but the producer did, and paid each a hefty salary. During the run one player came to Lerner & Loewe and announced the other bagpipes player was sick and couldn't go on that evening. "Can't you blow harder?" Lerner asked. "No one can tell the difference between the sound of one bagpipes playing, or two." The horrified player demurred; he couldn't go on alone. "Why not? You're getting paid enough!" shouted an exasperated Loewe. The player gulped: "I don't know how to play the bagpipes; I've been faking it and the other guy's been covering for me since opening night."

# 1952–1953

Winter Garden
Opened Wednesday, February 25, 1953
Robert Fryer presents:

## Wonderful Town

Book by Joseph Fields and Jerome Chodorov; Music by Leonard Bernstein; Lyrics by Betty Comden and Adolph Green; Dances and Musical Numbers staged by Donald Saddler; Sets and Costumes by Raoul Pene du Bois; Lighting by Peggy Clark; Based on the play *My Sister Eileen* and the stories by Ruth McKenney; Production directed by George Abbott.
*Cast*: Rosalind Russell, Edith Adams.

Composer, author, pianist, and conductor Leonard Bernstein's first stage experience was his jazz-oriented score for Jerome Robbins' ballet *Fancy Free* which then became *On the Town*, a Broadway musical comedy adapted by newcomers Betty Comden and Adolph Green. Bernstein was the wonderboy of this creaky adaptation of Chodorov and Fields' play. A trained musician in a field of gifted but mostly unstudied songwriters, Lenny was an anomaly who could write his own dance music and orchestrations. (His eclectic range of musical interests would ultimately frustrate his theatre career—but more about that later.) Comden and Green started in the business writing special material for their act *The*

*Revuers*, featuring Judy Holiday; so when *Wonderful Town*, starring Roz Russell, came along, Bernstein and Comden & Green were considered ideal collaborators for the comedienne. "One Hundred Easy Ways," sung in a spirit of self-mockery by the character Ruth Sherwood (Russell), could easily have been written for a cabaret act at the Village Vanguard or Blue Angel. Bernstein was canny enough to set the score to corny, funny tunes, as in "The Wrong Note Rag" with its old-fashioned blaring introduction and circa 1913 ragtime style melody. *Candide* and *West Side Story* would later confirm his musical genius, but for the moment he wrote formula melodies for such songs as "It's Love," "Pass the Football," "Conga!" and "Ohio." Lenny: why oh why oh?

---

Sam S. Shubert Theatre
Opened Thursday, May 7, 1953
Feuer and Martin present:

# Can-Can

Music and Lyrics by Cole Porter; Book and Direction by Abe Burrows; Dances and Musical Numbers staged by Michael Kidd; Setting and Lighting by Jo Mielziner; Costumes by Motley.
*Cast*: Lilo, Gwen Verdon, Hans Conried.

Lots of legs, behinds, black stockings, and bawdy Burrows jokes kept the tired businessman coming to see *Can-Can*, but an unknown, Gwen Verdon, who stole the show with Michael Kidd's great dance number, "The Garden of Eden," was the only element of the musical the critics would praise. Although *Can-Can* did not achieve the quality of *Kiss Me Kate*, his masterpiece, Porter's precious gift for songwriting was just as constant in 1953. The Paris setting inspired "I Love Paris" and "C'est Magnifique" for the francophile in us, and served to enrich Maurice Chevalier's repertoire. He could still be playful, asking in "I Am in Love": "should I order cyanide / Or merely champagne?" but the pièce de résistance in this Broadway fête was "It's All Right with Me." Unrequited love is painful, but leave it to Porter to find something piquant to say about the duplicity of men: "You can't know how happy I am that we met / I'm strangely attracted to you / There's someone I'm trying so hard to forget / Don't you want to forget someone too?" The emotion is universal and although it would have been scandalous in the fifties to suggest a woman could have the same ambivalent feelings, think of Madonna singing: "They're not his lips, but they're such tempting lips / That if some night you're free / Dear it's all right / It's all right with me." Of course.

Ira Gershwin thought lyrics should be ordinary conversation that rhymed, but Cole Porter was out of the commonplace and into the rare. The combination of Cole Porter's sophistication, humor, melody, rhyme, and intellect has rarely been equaled by another Broadway songwriter. From 1934 to 1938, before the so-called integrated song, where the lyric furthered the story (*Show Boat, Oklahoma!*), Porter was writing theatre songs for the fun of it, and for the joy and romance! They were posh, witty, risqué (but never vulgar), as with this double entendre in "My Heart Belongs to Daddy": "Though other dames / At football games / May long for a strong undergraddy / I never dream / Of making the team / 'Cause my heart belongs to daddy." Today's figure skaters perform a triple to win attention, but Porter was rhyming quadruples: "At words poetic / I'm so pathetic that I always have found it best / Instead of gettin'em off my chest / To let 'em rest / Unexpressed." He could show-off with "You're the Top" from *Anything Goes* as easily as he could be romantic, tender, even pensive, as in "Ev'rytime We Say Goodbye," a gorgeous song from *Seven Lively Arts*.

I first met Mr. Porter during a performance of *The Most Happy Fella*, when he had to be carried out of the Imperial Theatre due to complications from the recent amputation of his leg, culminating nearly twenty years of chronic pain he had suffered from a serious riding accident. "Please tell Frankie it wasn't his show but my indisposition that compelled me to leave," he implored in a tiny, childlike voice. It was the first time I had heard the word, indisposition, and promised myself to check the dictionary before conveying his message. Cole Porter songs never complain; they're optimistic even when saying good-bye ("Just One of Those Things"), so I wasn't too surprised to learn he defined his excruciating pain as a slight disorder.

# 1953–1954

Ziegfeld Theatre
Opened Thursday, December 3, 1953
Charles Lederer presents Edwin Lester's production of:

## *Kismet*

Music and Lyrics by Robert Wright and George Forrest; Music based on themes of Borodin; Musical Adaptation and Book by Charles Lederer and Luther Davis; Based on a play by Edward Knoblock; Production directed by Albert Marre; Dances and Musical Numbers staged by Jack Cole; Settings and Costumes designed by Lemuel Ayers; Lighting by Peggy Clark.
*Cast*: Alfred Drake, Joan Diener, Richard Kiley, Doretta Morrow.

*Kismet* was a vastly entertaining hybrid. Robert Wright and George Forrest, who first adapted and put lyrics to Edvard Grieg's music for *Song of Norway*, this time chose Borodin's music to convey the Arabian Nights atmosphere of Baghdad. It was an inspired collaboration. (The gentlemanly gifted Bob and Chet wrote their own music for the Broadway hit *Grand Hotel*.) Jack Cole's exotic dances and Lem Ayers' lush design gave the musical its style, but it was the towering performance of Alfred Drake, playing Hajj, the public poet, that astonished. It's fitting that I described Cole Porter paraphrasing a Wright and Forrest lyric. They can trade rhymes with the top, as demonstrated in "Rhymes Have I": "Lays / That sing / With rhymes have I / Couplets that ring / Like chimes have I /

Songs of sense / And pertinence / In reference / To all events / And climes." Their extravagant, deeply felt lyrics translated well with Russian composer Alexander Borodin's florid romantic music. His symphonic "Polovtsian Dances" produced "He's in Love" and the hit song of 1953, "Stranger in Paradise." Borodin's "String Quartet in D" became "And This Is My Beloved" and "Baubles, Bangles and Beads"; "Fate" was inspired by his symphonic poem "In the Steppes of Central Asia." Performing *Kismet* requires great voices, so it's no wonder that it has become part of the repertoire of the New York City Opera.

Edwin Lester, the producer of *Kismet*, originated the Los Angeles Civic Light Opera Association in the forties as a booking house for touring Broadway musicals. Lester and Frank Loesser lived in the same New York hotel penthouse floor during the run of *Kismet*, much to Loesser's displeasure. Lester's arch-conservative audience had compelled him to censor some of Loesser's *Guys and Dolls* lyrics for the road company's tour in Los Angeles, and Frank wanted revenge. As a result, guests who visited Loesser were told to first ring Lester's adjacent suite doorbell and ask if it was Frank Loesser's apartment. Edwin Lester was furious and decided to ask Loesser to stop the harassment. One day, sharing a jam-packed elevator, Lester sidled close to Loesser and whispered: "You're a great songwriter, Frank, and I'm a respected producer; why can't we act like colleagues?" Without missing a beat Loesser shouted: "If you touch me again I'll call a cop! And where is my laundry?" Everyone, except Frank, got off at the next floor. Call it destiny, fate; I call it kismet.

---

St. James Theatre

Opened Thursday, May 13, 1954

Frederick Brisson, Robert E. Griffith, and Harold S. Prince present:

# The Pajama Game

Book by George Abbott and Richard Bissell; Based on novel *7½ Cents* by Richard Bissell; Music and Lyrics by Richard Adler and Jerry Ross;

Scenery and Costumes by Lemuel Ayers; Choreography by Bob Fosse;
Production directed by George Abbott and Jerome Robbins.
*Cast*: Janis Paige, John Raitt, Carol Haney, Eddie Foy, Jr.

Frank Loesser nurtured Richard Adler's and Jerry Ross' career by signing them to his publishing company, Frank Music Corp. They immedi-
ately wrote four songs for *John Murray Anderson's Almanac* and had a
million-seller recording of their hit "Rags to Riches" with Tony Bennett.
When George Abbott was looking for songwriters for his next musical,
*The Pajama Game*, Loesser recommended Adler and Ross to the producers,
Freddie Brisson (Rosalind Russell's husband, who Frank named "the lizard
of Roz") and stage manager-turned-producer Hal Prince. Frank Music
Corp. was fast becoming a salon for Broadway composers and lyricists—
Adler & Ross, Wright & Forrest, Moose Charlap (and Meredith Willson
to come), and of course Loesser himself, with *Where's Charley?* and *Guys
and Dolls*. It was bedlam at 119 West 57th Street in New York; one team
of writers followed another into the only piano room on the floor. You
could hear Carolyn Leigh and Charlap (who were writing *Peter Pan*) caw-
ing "I've Got to Crow" all the way down the block to the Russian Tea
Room, and listen at the locked door to Loesser composing "Project #3,"
a code name for *The Most Happy Fella*. It was in this creative incubator
that Adler and Ross flourished.

The ability to both define character and be funny in a song is a gift
from the gods. Loesser, one of the theatre's brightest practitioners, passed
the torch to his protégés, and Adler and Ross wrote "I'll Never Be Jealous
Again" for vaudevillian Eddie Foy, Jr., in *The Pajama Game*. A middle-
aged man in love with a gorgeous younger woman celebrates the end of
his obsessive jealously after listening to two lurid examples of her possible
infidelity. "Well, Heinzie?" asks the inquisitor. Hines replies: "I would
trust her / There will be no more nightmares to sleep through / No more
bushes to creep through!" He is sorely tested a third time, with a gentle
schottische sung by his doubting tormentor: "Picture this, you go to your
sweetie's apartment / You borrowed the keys / There she is / She's giving
a sailor / A very affectionate squeeze / Then to boot / She tells you she
was in the arms of her cousin / Who's back from overseas." Hines hits
the ceiling: "*Her cousin from overseas! Do you expect me to believe that?*"
Inquisitor: "Heinzie?" Then in a heartbeat, catching himself in mid-air,
Hines recants: "I would trust her"; and vows seventeen times never to be
jealous again. Wanna bet?

"Hey There," "Hernando's Hideaway," "Steam Heat," "I'm Not at all in Love," "Small Talk," and three other show-stoppers launched the creators of *The Pajama Game* into the next Broadway era. Fosse's choreography, executed by Carol Haney, Peter Gennaro, Buzz Miller and a new gypsy in the chorus, Shirley MacLaine, was sensational. Musically, "Hernando's Hideaway" is a composite of every Argentine tango from "Jealousy" and "La Paloma" to Bizet's "Habanera Song." Adler and Ross' pastiche references to dark secluded places, fast embraces, castanets, and knocking three times make us imagine stealthy dances and furtive glances, and also make us smile. "Steam Heat" was the dance number that made Fosse famous, but it was the ingenuity of Adler and Ross' percussion blasts (Clang! Clang!) on the radiator followed by two beats of sibilant sound—"Ssssssssteam heat"—that gave the number its unique signature. (As with some audiences who believe the actors make up their dialogue, choreographers tend to forget it is the composer who creates their dances on music manuscript paper.) "Hey There" proved to be a popular hit song on the airways, in spite of a gimmicky stage device. John Raitt sings his thoughts into a Dictaphone and performs a duet with himself during the playback. It was a nightmare for the conductor—who had pre-recorded the orchestral accompaniment and Raitt's second chorus of "Hey There"—and for eight performances a week, in precisely the same tempo, he began the first chorus live on stage, dropped the pit orchestra out after the bridge, played the tape, and cued the live orchestra and Raitt back in for the final six bars. Another less technical but equally challenging problem was the leading lady, Janis Paige. (The experience helped me direct her in *Here's Love.*) During *The Pajama Game* tryout rehearsal in the Taft Hotel, New Haven, George Abbott directed Janis to exit a scene earlier than she wanted. Exasperated, she asked: "What is my motivation?" Abbott replied: "We open Saturday night."

When composer Jerry Ross died unexpectedly after their second smash hit, *Damn Yankees*, Alder tried writing both words and music but the chemistry wasn't the same. No one really knows why a successful collaboration works. I like to think of collaboration as group sculpture, the passing of clay back and forth to create a face; one person molds the head, another the mouth, the nose, and so on. It doesn't make any difference who and how much each collaborator contributes, it's the final creation that counts. During *The Pajama Game* Dick and Jerry were closeted in the same Taft Hotel, with second act problems. Fosse had asked for a big new dance number, a tango, for Carol Haney. It was past midnight and nothing was coming. "Olay . . ." said Ross in mock desperation to Adler. "Thanks a lot," Adler mumbled. Finally, an exhausted Adler spoke: "The only thing I can think of is a title—Hernando's Hideaway." "Why that?" asked Ross. "Because it rhymes with Olay," Adler replied. They wrote the entire song in two hours: "I know a dark secluded place / A place where no one knows your face / A glass of wine, a fast embrace / It's called Hernando's hideaway; / Olay!" Chemistry.

---

Theatre De Lys
Opened Wednesday, March 19, 1954
Carmen Capalbo and Stanley Chase present:

# The Threepenny Opera

English adaptation of books and lyrics by Marc Blitzstein; Music by Kurt Weill; Original text by Bertolt Brecht; Staged by Carmen Capalbo. *Cast:* Jo Sullivan, Scott Merrill, Beatrice Arthur, Lotte Lenya, Charlotte Ray.

This production, although it premiered off-Broadway, was significant in many respects. It ran for 2,611 performances and was exquisitely produced. Kurt Weill, one of the few trained musicians who composed for Broadway ("My Ship" from *Lady in the Dark*, "Speak Low" from *One Touch of Venus*, "September Song" from *Knickerbocker Holiday*) originally collaborated with Brecht on *Dreigroschenoper*, the 1928 updated German version of John Gay's *The Beggar's Opera*. Marc Blitzstein, another well-educated opera composer (*Regina, The Cradle Will Rock*), translated, adapted, and wrote the lyrics for the revival, now entitled *The Threepenny Opera*. Many of Weill's theatre songs, including "Mack the Knife" have become standards. His catalog of music alternates between classical and popular, sinister and haunting, simple and complex. (For "My Ship," written with Ira Gershwin as connective tissue for the four stories that comprise *Lady in the Dark*, he composed a child-like melody to dramatize a troubled adult's dreams.) He was Germany's George Gershwin, trained to compose symphonies while playing piano in kinky cafés and learning about the songs of the day. The uncompromising repeat of sixteen measures for seven choruses in "Mack the Knife" is not easy listening, but its wit, pathos, and sardonic echoes of the murderous underworld cannot be ignored. The musical's cynical, tongue-in-cheek, satirical nature was brilliantly realized by a cast of new faces: Jo Sullivan (later to star in *The Most Happy Fella*), Bea Arthur (of *Maude* television fame), and Lotte Lenya, Weill's wife, who added the essential ethnic authenticity to the production.

## OTHER MUSICALS

*The Girl in Pink Tights*, with music by Sigmund Romberg and lyrics by Leo Robin, contributed "Lost In Loveliness" (and little else), while John Latouche and Jerome Moross enchanted us with "Lazy Afternoon" in *The Golden Apple* to end the season. (It was one of those rare lyrics that define the art: "It's a lazy afternoon / And the beetle bugs are zoomin' / And the tulip trees are bloomin' / And there's not another human in view / And I know a place that's quiet 'cept for daisies running riot / And there's no one passing by it to see.") About this time another master-to-be, Stephen Sondheim, was writing his first musical with the Epsteins—*Saturday Night*.

# 1954–1955

Imperial Theatre
Opened Thursday, February 24, 1955
Feuer and Martin present:

## Silk Stockings

Music and Lyrics by Cole Porter; Book by George S. Kaufman, Leueen MacGrath and Abe Burrows; Suggested by *Ninotchka* by Melchoir Lengyel; Setting and Lighting by Jo Mielziner; Costumes by Lucinda Ballard; Dances and Musical Numbers staged by Eugene Loring; Directed by Cy Feuer.

*Cast*: Don Ameche, Hildergarde Neff, George Tobias, Gretchen Wyler.

Cole Porter's lyric for "All of You" in *Silk Stockings* had all the sexual overtones necessary to seduce a cold Ninotchka: "I love the looks of you / The lure of you / The sweet of you / The pure of you / The eyes, the arms, the mouth of you / The East, West, North, and the South of you." It was his siren-song to Broadway, and was never more appropriate than for this deadly rip-off of Garbo's classic film. *Silk Stockings* stayed out of town thirteen weeks for repairs (an unheard of amount of time then) and is evidence of Feuer and Martin's producing savvy. These pros knew how to save a show. They beefed up a number for leggy chorine Gretchen Wyler ("Stereophonic Sound"), had sexier chorus girl costumes designed, called in Abe Burrows to doctor the limp book and help director Feuer get laughs from top comic actors David Opatoshu, Leon Belasco, and Henry Lascoe. They even got Porter to rewrite "Siberia" until it stopped the show. The combination of a hit song, a memorable story, the name value of the creators, and lots of money spent on scenery and costumes resulted in a long, albeit undeserved, run. Andrew Lloyd Webber was only seven years old at the time.

———————

Forty-Sixth Street Theatre
Opened Thursday, May 5, 1955
Frederick Brisson, Robert E. Griffith, and Harold S. Prince in association with Albert B. Taylor present:

# Damn Yankees

Book by George Abbott and Douglas Wallop; Music and Lyrics by Richard Adler and Jerry Ross; Based on the novel *The Year the Yankees Lost the Pennant* by Douglas Wallop; Dances and Musical Numbers staged by Bob Fosse; Scenery and Costumes designed by William and Jean Eckart; Production directed by George Abbott.
*Cast*: Gwen Verdon, Ray Walston, Stephen Douglas, Robert Shafer.

George Abbott always started a new show the day after opening night (a tradition Hal Prince was to emulate) and after *The Pajama Game* opened Adler & Ross were immediately recruited to collaborate on *Damn Yankees*. They proved their successful rookie debut wasn't a fluke by writing "Whatever Lola Wants," "Heart," "Who's Got the Pain?" "Two Lost Souls," and "Those Were the Good Old Days." The heavy-hitting score provided a field day for a first-rate team—Ray Walston, Jimmie Komack, Russ Brown, Nat Frey, and especially Gwen Verdon.

"Those Were the Good Old Days" increased their comedy-character batting average, this time for a slick operator who says he's Applegate, but we know he's the devil: "I see cannibals munchin' a missionary luncheon / The years may have flown / But the mem'ry stays / Like the hopes that were dashed / When the stock market crashed" (then with a languid trombone lick reminiscent of vaudevillian Ted Lewis), "Ha, ha, ha, ha,

/ Those were the good old days." Add a tag, paraphrasing Jolson's "Mammy": "I'd walk a million miles or more / For some of the gore / Of those good old days!" and you have a show-stopper. Everybody was happy. Bob Fosse was, especially with "Who's Got the Pain," another comedy number and a dance for Gwen Verdon and Eddie Phillips. This special material had nothing to do with the plot but had audiences jumping from their seats, grunting, "*Ugh*" each time the song asked, "Who's got the pain when they do the mambo / Who's got the pain when they go / '*Ugh*'?" Latin rhythms were lucky for Adler & Ross. First, an Argentine tango ("Hernando's Hideaway"), then a Cuban mambo ("Pain"), and lastly a Spanish bolero ("Whatever Lola Wants"). Joe Hardy didn't stand a chance when Lola vamped: "I always get what I aim for / And your heart and soul is what I came for." (A seduction of another kind, with homage to Porter's "All of You.") Richard Adler and Jerry Ross were a songwriting team with their heads in musical theatre and their hearts in vaudeville. There is no better example than "Heart," their soft-shoe-barbershop-quartet tribute to the great American pastime, baseball: "You can open any door / There's noth'in to it / But to do it / You've gotta have/H-e-a-r-t."

## OTHER MUSICALS

*Damn Yankees* was the smash hit everyone was rooting for in this season of (extraordinary) near misses: *The Boy Friend*, introducing Julie Andrews singing "A Room in Bloomsbury"; Jerome Robbins' *Peter Pan*, with Mary Martin's "I'm Flying" and "Neverland"; Harold Rome's *Fanny*, with Ezio Pinza; Gian-Carlo Menotti's *The Saint of Bleeker Street* (which won the Drama Critics Award and the Pulitzer Prize); *House of Flowers*, by Harold Arlen and Truman Copote, with "A Sleeping Bee" and "Two Ladies in de Shade of de Banana Tree"; and *Plain and Fancy*, with Barbara Cook and the hit song "Young and Foolish." All came close, but no cigar. One can't emphasize enough the value of a hit song in a Broadway musical. Free radio and television air play was a constant commercial, reminding audiences the song came from a show they had to see. Broadway melodies were played at weddings, bar-mitzvahs, proms, football games, parades, and on the Astor Roof on New Year's Eve in Times Square. All this would disappear in a few years, when rock'n'roll changed the style of popular music, signaling the decline of the Broadway musical.

# 1955–1956

Mark Hellinger Theatre
Opened Thursday, March 15, 1956
Herman Levin presents:

## My Fair Lady

Book and Lyrics by Alan Jay Lerner; Adapted from Bernard Shaw's
*Pygmalion*; Music by Frederick Loewe; Staged by Moss Hart; Choreography and Musical Numbers by Hanya Holm; Designed by Oliver Smith;
Costumes by Cecil Beaton; Lighting by Feder.
*Cast*: Rex Harrison, Julie Andrews, Robert Coote, Stanley Holloway,
Cathleen Nesbit.

In April 1956 both *My Fair Lady* and *The Most Happy Fella* were trying
out in Philadelphia, en route to Broadway. Frank Loesser and I went to
the Earlanger Theatre to see the Lerner and Loewe musical and check
out the competition. It was clearly a box-office bonanza and one of the
best musicals ever produced. Frank turned to me after the final curtain
and said: "The pain is plain and mainly in my brain; I think they've got
it." Indeed, they had. *My Fair Lady* was the zenith of musical theatre
writing for its time: "I've Grown Accustomed to Her Face," "I Could
Have Danced All Night," "On the Street Where You Live," "The Rain
in Spain," "Show Me," "Get Me to the Church on Time," and "With a

Little Bit of Luck" all became standards of musical theatre exhilaration and enriched the worldwide affection for Broadway musicals.

"It's 'Awoo' and 'G'arn' that keeps her in her place; not her wretched cloths or dirty face," says Professor Henry Higgins, referring to a coarse cockney girl selling flowers in London's Covent Garden. "Awoo, wouldn't it be loverly," Eliza sings, dropping her H's so that "heat" becomes "eat" and "head," "ed." Lerner's uncanny ear for dialect is ab-so-bloomin-lutely brilliant in "Wouldn't It Be Loverly," an impoverished girl's plaintive plea for the small comforts of life, and the first of many *My Fair Lady* songs in love with language. Loewe understood his music shouldn't compete with his partner's syntax and composed deceptively simple melodies with an octave range, leaving the performer the freedom to act the lyric rather than coping with difficult musical intervals. "Just You Wait" does exactly that, in a march-tempo 4/4 dirge, as Eliza plans her revenge for Higgins' condescending manner and heartless teaching methods. As comic relief, Loewe also gives Eliza a mock-soprano interlude to demonstrate her bravura ability. Charming.

The wager Higgins has made with Pickering—that he can teach this cockney wretch to speak proper English—is about to be forfeited when Eliza (in another of the great moments of Broadway theatre), instead of saying, "rine" and "Spine," utters her first A correctly:

*Eliza*: The rain in Spain stays mainly in the plain.

*Higgins*: What was that?

*Eliza*: The rain in Spain stays mainly in the plain.

*Higgins*: Again.

(A Habanera sneaks in, to accompany the dialogue.)

*Eliza*: The rain in Spain stays mainly in the plain.

*Higgins*: I think she's got it! I think she's got it!

(Eliza sings:) "The rain in Spain stays mainly in the plain."

*Higgins*: By George she's got it! By George she's got it!

Higgins sings: "Now once again, where does it rain?" "On the plain!" she replies, and the Habanera increases in tempo and swells in volume: "And where's that soggy plain?" Higgins shouts, sensing the enormity of his accomplishment. Eliza replies triumphantly: "In Spain! In Spain!" And the stage explodes! Pickering, Higgins and Eliza dance a flamenco, mime a bullfighter's kill, and sweep us along into an ecstatic celebration of her transformation. Now that she's become Cinderella and speaks the King's English, Eliza cannot sleep: "Not for all the jewels in the crown / I could have danced all night." Lerner and Loewe, again in love with dialect, set the word 'jew-els' to two notes to make it sound upper-class, and repeat the word "danced" six times so we may revel in Eliza's ability to stress her A's, as in "I could have 'dhaaanced' all night." "Words, words, words / I'm so sick of words / I get words all day through / First from him, now from you / Is that all you blighters can do?" Yes, Eliza, and they can do it with the speed of summer lightning, as in the furious waltz "Show Me." George Bernard Shaw would have rolled over at the thought of Higgins singing the sentimental "I've Grown Accustomed To Her Face" if not for the fortune his estate was earning from *My Fair Lady*. So in the end Lerner and Loewe were permitted to tag on a happy ending to *Pygmalion*, with a begrudging confession yet tender concession to love.

The original cast album of *My Fair Lady* was the first to sell a million records and was produced by the show's benefactor, Goddard Leiberson, who convinced CBS to finance the entire production. (Leiberson was to continue pouring investment capital into Broadway, including three of my early solo productions: *We Take the Town*, *Here's Love*, and *The Apple Tree*.) America's historical intimidation by and fascination for anything English released the public's repressed desires and adulation for London travel, Saville Row suits, Bernard Shaw's letters, Ascot Races, Cecil Beaton designs, and most of all, Rex Harrison and Julie Andrews, whom they crowned King and Queen of Broadway. Indeed, America's *My Fair Lady* repaid England for the loss of her colonies.

---

Imperial Theatre
Opened Thursday, May 3, 1956
Kermit Bloomgarden and Lynn Loesser present:

# The Most Happy Fella

By Frank Loesser; Based on Sidney Howard's play *They Knew What They Wanted*; Orchestrations by Don Walker; Choreography by Dania Krup-

ska; Scenery and Lighting by Jo Mielziner; Costumes by Motley; Directed by Joseph Anthony.
*Cast*: Robert Weede, Jo Sullivan, Art Lund, Susan Johnson.

When we opened out of town and the critics hailed *The Most Happy Fella* as a "brilliant new American opera," Loesser was horrified that the highbrow tone of the notices would scare away traditional Broadway audiences. "Call the press, Ostrow, and tell 'em we're not an opera for God's sake; we're a . . . Loessercal!" Ironically, Frank was insecure about his lack of music education notwithstanding his great Broadway successes—brought about in part by his perceived position in the Loesser family. His older brother, Arthur, was a celebrated pianist and an academician, and his mother was a cultured matriarch who thought being a Tin Pan Alley song writer was meretricious. All the more astonishing this self-taught composer was able to create a seminal opera/musical comedy/dramatico-musical work, which has endured and promises to be around past the millennium.

The truth is the score for *The Most Happy Fella* is a cornucopia of operatic arias ("My Heart Is So Full of You"), Hit Parade songs ("Standing on the Corner") and other musical expressions that cannot be defined. "Ooh! My Feet!" is just such a phenomenon. Rather than a flashy happy opening number danced and sung by a chorus of Broadway gypsies, Loesser begins the musical with a solitary barefoot waitress massaging her foot: "This little piggy feels the weight of the plate / Tho' the freight's just an order of Melba toast / And this little piggy is the littlest little piggy / But the big son of a bitch hurts the most!" Possibly because Susan Johnson had a voice like a room full of cellos, or due to the sheer impertinence of the song, audiences stopped the show each performance when she finished with: "I've been on my feet / My poor poor feet / All day long today / Doin' my blue plate special ballet!" "Somebody, Somewhere," a beautiful soprano lament, followed, setting the musical's operatic tone: "Somebody lonely wants me to care / Wants me of all people / To notice him there / Well I want to be wanted / Need to be needed."

"Big D" and "I Like Everybody" had little to do with the plot but were vastly entertaining and written as contrast to the seriousness of the entire work. It is testimony to Frank Loesser's immense talent that *The Most Happy Fella* never broke down with schizophrenia. In a sense Loesser wrote enough music for two shows: ballads—"Joey, Joey, Joey," "Don't Cry," "Warm All Over"; choral numbers—"The Most Happy Fella," Sposalizio," "Fresno Beauties," "How Beautiful the Days," "Song of a

Summer Night"; arias—"A Long Time Ago," "Plenty Bambini," "Young People," "I Know How It Is," "Aren't You Glad?" "I Don't Like This Dame," "Like a Woman Loves a Man," "Please Let Me Tell You"; duets—"Happy To Make Your Acquaintance," "Cold and Dead"; and trios—"Abbondanza," "Benvenuta," "Nobody's Ever Gonna Love You"; the sheer numbers prompted Columbia Records to record its first three-set Original Cast Album, at a running time of 134:12.

I first met my wife-to-be, Ann Gilbert, on the opening night of *The Most Happy Fella* in the Imperial Theatre lobby and was in love with her by the second act. This may explain why I well up each time I hear, "Mamma, Mamma," Tony's curtain soliloquy to end act two. Tony's betrothed, Rosabella, has just learned she is pregnant, but not by him. Oblivious of events, Tony looks up towards the stars: "Mamma, Mamma, up in heaven / How you like my girl? / How you like your dumb, funny lookin' boy? / He was wait-a so long / He's a-a finda-a such joy / An' I'm feel-a so young / An' I'm a feel-a so strong / An' I'm a feel-a so smart! / Tell-a me Mamma, Mamma, up in heaven / How you like-a my sweetheart?" Gulp. The anecdote: Morley Meredith was originally cast as Joe, but after the Boston opening Loesser wanted a pop voice to croon "Don't Cry" and "Joey, Joey, Joey"; he sent for Art Lund, a former Benny Goodman band singer, to replace Meredith for the Philadelphia opening. Meredith didn't have an adequate understudy so the producers, fearing he would find out he was being replaced and quit before Lund was ready to go on, rehearsed Lund in the Warwick Hotel ballroom far away from the Shubert Theatre. It was a mad rush to get him in the part, so on opening night when Lund was supposed to sing: "And the wind blows in / Smelling of Oregon cherries," Art instead sang, "Smelling of ordinary women." The next day the *Philadelphia Inquirer* wrote: "Art Lund's delivery of 'Joey, Joey, Joey' was thrilling, with the exception of one lapse of taste which should have been banned in Boston."

# 1956–1957

Sam S. Shubert Theatre
Opened Thursday, November 1956
The Theatre Guild presents:

## Bells Are Ringing

Book and Lyrics by Betty Comden and Adolph Green; Music by Jule
Styne; Entire Production directed by Jerome Robbins; Sets and Cos-
tumes by Raoul Pene du Bois; Lighting by Peggy Clark; Dances and
Musical Numbers staged by Jerome Robbins and Bob Fosse.
*Cast*: Judy Holliday, Sydney Chaplin.

Notice how many Broadway shows opened on a Thursday night? Here's
why. Previews would begin on Monday and conventional thinking was
by Thursday the cast and crew would be primed to give their best performance—a mixture of adrenaline and magic. Furthermore, a rave notice
in the Friday morning newspapers would spur off-work weekend ticket
buying. (In the sixties when the *New York Times* drama critic insisted on
coming to previews in order to have more time to write his notice, the
tradition of one make-or-break opening night performance became mean-
ingless, and the theatre lost its soul.)

Jule Styne and Frank Loesser both came to Broadway via Tin Pan
Alley. They collaborated once ("I Don't Want to Walk Without You"),
when Loesser was writing lyrics for Paramount Pictures. Styne was a lov-

able mug, a fast talker ("You're a hundred percent right kid, except for one thing"), an inveterate horse player, and a ladies' man. Nathan Detroit with talent. His scores for *High Button Shoes*, with Sammy Cahn, and *Gentleman Prefer Blondes*, with Leo Robin, were overshadowed by Jerome Robbins' *Keystone Kops Ballet* and Carol Channing, respectively; but when he wrote *Bells Are Ringing* with Comden and Green he was a force on Broadway. He was fortunate to have Judy Holliday as his star to deliver "The Party's Over," "It's a Perfect Relationship," and "I'm Going Back." Sidney Chaplin was swarthy and sweet (a characterization he was to repeat in *Funny Girl*, another Jule Styne hit), and his husky delivery of the number one Hit Parade song of 1956, "Just in Time," kept *Bells Are Ringing* running for years.

Music came easy to Styne, and he so loved writing for the theatre he accepted almost every show offered to him, often with disastrous results: *Two on the Aisle, Hazel Flagg, Say Darling, Subways Are for Sleeping, Fade Out–Fade In, Hallelujah Baby, Darling of the Day, Look to the Lilies, Sugar,* and *The Red Shoes*. Nevertheless there was always one great tune from each show to be celebrated, as in *Do Re Mi*—an effortless melody entitled "Make Someone Happy." For *Peter Pan* (a Charlap-Leigh show they were called in to doctor) Styne wrote a glorious melody with an octave and five note range (duck soup for Mary Martin), "Neverland."

*Bells Are Ringing* was the most fruitful of the Styne / Comden and Green collaborations. In this, yet another Cinderella story variation, Ella runs a telephone answering service (Bells) and is in love with Jeff's voice: "I'm in love / With a man / Plaza oh double four double three / It's a perfect relationship / I can't see him / He can't see me." Finally she fakes a phony identity and in a fairy tale moment, when musical theatre takes you off the ground, he asks her to dance:

> *Ella*: In the park?
>
> *Jeff*: What's the matter? No guts?
>
> (He starts dancing her across the stage)
>
> *Ella*: Stop it.

He sings, "Just in time / I found you just in time / Before you came my time was running low." And the song becomes a standard in the Broadway canon. Ella must face the truth that Jeff is in love with a girl who doesn't exist and resigns herself: "The party's over / It's time to call it a day."

Tragically, it was also over for Judy Holliday nine years after starring in *Bells Are Ringing*. She was only forty-three when she died.

---

Martin Beck Theatre
Opened Saturday, December 1, 1956
Ethel Linder Reiner in association with Lester Osterman, Jr., presents:

# Candide

Book by Lillian Hellman; Based on Voltaire's satire; Score by Leonard Bernstein; Lyrics by Richard Wilber; Other Lyrics by John LaTouche and Dorothy Parker; Designed by Oliver Smith; Costumes by Irene Sharaff; Lighting by Paul Morrison; Directed by Tyrone Guthrie assisted by Tom Brown. Dance Supervisors: Wallace Seibert, Anna Sokolow. *Cast*: Barbara Cook, Max Adrian, Robert Rounseville, Irra Petina.

*Candide* was a glorious mess. Bernstein's music was the glorious part. The show's messy billing was a tip-off to the cognoscente—three different lyricists, two directors, and two dance supervisors suggest that all the creators, other than Bernstein, either needed help or didn't want to accept full credit, or blame, for the musical as a whole. Bernstein's music is indestructible, notwithstanding the many attempts to produce a successful version of Voltaire's masterpiece. It's no accident Bernstein's overture to *Candide* is the most thrilling in the canon. (Jule Styne's *Gypsy* is second.) The reason? There are no lyrics. Leonard Bernstein's musical erudition and comedic flair was never more apparent than in "Oh Happy We" and Cunegonde's "Glitter and Be Gay," a send-up of "The Jewel Song" from the opera *Faust*. His eclectic range of musical interests and appetite for living would ultimately frustrate his theatre career. He would begin a musical, turn to composing a celebrant's *Mass*, or dash off a clarinet con-certo, all at the same time.

The best musical (on paper) I ever produced was *A Pray by Blecht*, one of those Bernstein musicals interrupted by excess. Jerome Robbins came to me in 1967 with Brecht's *The Exception and the Rule*, a lehrstücke/teaching lesson typical of the German playright's preoccupation with the struggle of the masses. The story was about a merchant and a coolie and how the merchant exploited the lower classes. It was Jerry's and Leonard Bernstein's notion to juxtapose the musical's theme with black and white race relations. I brought in Jerry Leiber to write the lyrics, John Guare to write the book, and Zero Mostel to play the merchant. (Stephen Sondheim was momentarily persuaded to join the project after hearing Guare's idea of turning the musical into a live-on-the-air telecast.) Possibly due to the "radical chic" syndrome, as Tom Wolfe labeled it, or the fact that five white middle-class New Yorkers knew little about the suffering of the black man in the sixties, the project bogged down. I suggested we hire *Dutchman's* black dramatist, Leroi Jones/Imamu Amiri Baraka, to help us. Mr. Baraka would have nothing to do with us. By this time Sondheim had withdrawn, Lenny was in Vienna planning Mahler's Philharmonic resurrection, and out of desperation Arthur Laurents was asked to play-doctor. It was too much firepower too late, and I decided not to continue as producer. Years later Robbins revived the project with Josh Mostel (Zero's son), and it was just as wrongheaded. *A Pray by Blecht* suffered from an excess of self-righteousness and talent.

# 1957–1958

Winter Garden
Opened Thursday, September 26, 1957
Robert E. Griffith and Harold S. Prince (by arrangement with
Roger L. Stevens) present:

## West Side Story

Book by Arthur Laurents; Music by Leonard Bernstein; Lyrics by Steven
Sondheim; Entire Production directed by Jerome Robbins; Scenic Pro-
duction by Oliver Smith; Costumes by Irene Sharaff; Lighting by Jean
Rosenthal; Co-Choreographer Peter Gennaro.
*Cast*: Carol Lawrence, Larry Kurt, Chita Rivera.

Jerry Robbins conceived *West Side Story* as a ballet with songs and
dialogue. One must pay tribute to author Arthur Laurents for what he
left out of the *Romeo and Juliet*–inspired book in order to accommodate
Robbins' concept. Robbins became Broadway's preeminent Director/
Choreographer, inspiring Bob Fosse, Gower Champion, and Michael
Bennett to follow in his dance steps. (It also afforded Robbins a box
around his billing—a first.) Even the chorus members of the original
production of *West Side Story* were special: Grover Dale (Snowboy),
Tommy Abbott (Gee-Tar), and Lee Becker (Anybodys) became Broad-
way choreographers; Martin Charnin (Big Deal) later wrote and directed
*Annie*; Reri Grist went on to the Metropolitan Opera; and Marilyn Coo-

per was soon to be a featured comedienne in a dozen new musicals and plays.

The most significant debut however was that of the show's lyricist, 27-year-old Stephen Sondheim. A composer in his own right, it wouldn't be until *A Funny Thing Happened on the Way to the Forum* that Steve would be asked to write both words and music. Oscar Hammerstein was Sondheim's mentor. (As George Abbott was Hal Prince's and Frank Loesser, mine.) Ironically, the master Hammerstein was the eternal optimist, and pupil Sondheim—with his fierce intelligence, command of language, and questioning outlook on life—the pessimist. His lyric to "Somewhere" is evermore ironic when you consider that the dispossessed West Side gang members in this story haven't a chance: "Someday, somewhere / We'll find a new way of living / We'll find a way of forgiving." Sure.

Leonard Bernstein's Symphony No. 2, *The Age of Anxiety*, for piano and orchestra, introduced his penchant for jazz rhythms, which he utilized handily in *West Side Story*'s "Something's Coming," which sets the anxious tone of the musical with its ice-cold jagged syncopation. With "Maria," one of the most beautiful sounds I ever heard was the transition from the introduction to the chorus of the song. One need not be musically literate to feel the tremendous lift when this occurs. At the turn of the century, Bert Williams' black shiftless layabout character singing "Nobody" and another vaudeville act's Jewish ridicule-question-and-answer signature song, "Mr. Gallagher and Mr. Shean," proved you could make fun of an ethnic sterotype, so long as you *were* the stereotype. (Sinbad and Jackie Mason are today's examples.) In 1957, it was *West Side Story*'s Anita, a Puerto Rican who makes fun of her own kind: "Always the hurricanes blowing / Always the population growing / And the money owing / And the babies crying / And the bullets flying / I like the island Manhattan / Smoke on your pipe and put that in!" If there was any doubt this musical was inspired by Shakespeare's play, one has only to compare: "Good Night Good Night! Parting is such sweet sorrow—That I shall say good night till it be morrow" to: "Oh moon grow bright / And make this endless day endless night!" No one more than Steve felt "I Feel Pretty" with its witty-pity, charming-alarming rhymes was out of place in a story concerning ethnic gang-war rivalry. Today it is used as a theme song by drag queens, but no matter; this nonpareil score will endure, and there is no better testimony to its greatness than "Somewhere," Bernstein's and Sondheim's anthem hope for humanity. As if to warn us of the difficulty of the road ahead they end the last chord of the song in a whisper, in a prayer.

The combination of Laurents, Robbins, Bernstein, and Sondheim, representing the most literate, experienced, educated, fresh, and artistic team of creators in the fifties, created a landmark musical. Its seriousness attracted a new generation of theatregoers and frightened the Broadway establishment, who gave the Tony Award for Best Musical that year to *The Music Man.*

---

Magestic Theatre
Opened December 19, 1957
Kermit Bloomgarden with Herbert Greene in association with Frank
Productions, Inc., present:

# The Music Man

Book, Music and Lyrics by Meredith Willson; Story by Meredith Willson and Franklin Lacey; Staged by Morton Da Costa; Choreography by Onna White; Settings and Lighting by Howard Bay; Costumes by Raoul Pene du Bois.
*Cast*: Robert Preston, Barbara Cook, David Burns, Pert Kelton.

You could say my journey with *The Music Man* began when I haunted the NBC radio studios in Rockefeller Center, especially Studio 8H where Toscanini conducted the NBC Symphony Orchestra, and where Meredith Willson conducted the orchestra and chorus for "The Big Show" starring Tallulah Bankhead. I was nineteen then; a clarinetist, vocal arranger and conductor—cocksure of being the next Fred Waring—having appeared with my chorus on NBC and CBS television's "Prize Performance," "Songs for Sale," "Horn and Hardart Hour," and "Wendy Barrie." The novelty of an adolescent conductor was wearing thin, however, when fate sounded its french horn and I was drafted. Remembering Meredith Willson was the WW2 head of Armed Forces Radio Service, I crashed Studio 8H, found Willson, and asked if he would recommend me for AFRS. He asked to see my vocal arrangements, and miraculously, liked them. Meredith's specialty at the time was "The Talking Men," a speak-song male chorus that spoke rhythmically (the device was to become famous when Willson wrote "Rock Island," the opening number for *The Music Man*), so not only did Willson give me the recommendation, he also put me to work writing vocal arrangements for the chorus. Three years later, after serving in the USAF, meeting Frank Loesser and joining his music publishing company, I was promoted to governor-general of Frank Music's west coast office, and contacted Willson who was living in West Los Angeles. As always, he was gracious and generous and asked if I would like to listen to his new musical, *The Silver Triangle*, which Feur and Martin had recently dropped. It was the second time that my relationship with a songwriter was to change my life. The musical was re-entitled *The Music Man*, Frank Music Corp. became the publisher, I was assigned to work on the score exclusively, and my journey took wings, or in this case, took tracks.

"You can talk / You can bicker / You can talk all you want to / But it's different than it was / But you gotta know the territory!" From the opening speak-song in the "Rock Island" railway coach for traveling salesmen, to the River City High School assembly hall finale where conman Harold Hill's promised "think system" is realized, Broadway audiences were entranced by Meredith Willson's valentine to 1912 Iowa and his lovable River City (read Mason City) characters. When Willson, fresh from Mason City, Iowa, first came to Chicago as a piccolo player in John Phillip Sousa's 1924 famous marching band and was handed a plate of a dozen oysters at a welcoming cocktail party, he didn't know what to make of them. Thirty minutes later the hostess returned and she noticed only one of the succulent oysters had been eaten; she asked him if he cared for the big city oysters. Meredith managed a crooked smile, and pointing to his puckered-clenched teeth, indicated to the hostess that he didn't even like the one he still held in his mouth. Three decades later, no longer a rube, he paid homage to the March King by writing this introduction for Harold Hill's "Seventy-Six Trombones" for *The Music Man*.

> And you'll see the glitter of crashing cymbals,
> And you'll hear the thunder of rolling drums, the
>     shimmer of trumpets—Tantara!
> And you'll feel something akin to the electric
>     thrill I once enjoyed
> When Gilmore, Liberatti, Pat Conway
> The Great Creatore, W. C. Handy
>     and John Philip Sousa
> All came to town on the very same historic day!

Then in a brisk 6/8 march tempo, announced by five drum ruffles and a blare of brass (Ba-ba-ba-ba-BAA-ba-ba-ba-BOOM! BOOM! BOOM!), Harold sings: "Seventy-six trombones led the big parade / With a hundred and ten cornets close at hand," and parades a thousand reeds, copper bottom timpani, double bell euphoniums, fifty mounted canon, and clarinets of every size into our imaginations. It tore the roof off the Majestic Theatre and if you didn't get up and march at the climax of this number you were either crippled or deaf. Willson wrote the word "Slam" to denote a rhythmic pause in his speak-songs. "Ya Got Trouble," for example, could be considered the progenitor of today's Rap and Hip-Hop.

(Slam) "Ya got Trouble—my friend,
(Slam) Right here, I say
Trouble right here in River
City. Why sure, I'm a
Billiard player, certainly
Mighty proud to say it
(Slam) I consider that the
Hours I spend with a
Cue in my hand are
Golden. (Slam)
(Slam) Help you cultivate
HORSE sense and a
COOL head and a
KEEN eye.
'Jever take and try to give an iron-clad leave to
yourself from a three-rail billiard shot?"

I recall *The Music Man* gypsy run-through—Broadway jargon for a private performance of a new musical attended by the cast members' family and friends on the last day of rehearsals before the out-of-town tryout. It was Robert Preston's first musical and he was struggling to read a revised lyric Willson had written the night before for "Ya Got Trouble." Everyone thought "Pres" would choke in front of his first, albeit friendly, audience, but instead he finished the song by throwing the sheet music in the air without missing a (Slam).

Meredith Willson was a consummate musician, pianist, composer, lyricist, conductor, and performer. He could write marches, barbershop quartets, speak-songs, ballads, and occasionally an aria, such as: "My white knight / Not a Lancelot nor an angel with wings / Just someone to love me / Who is not ashamed of a few nice things / And if occasion'ly he'd ponder / What makes Shakespeare and Beethoven great / Him I could love 'till I die," or a love song for a beguiled librarian, "There were bells on the hill but I never heard them ringing / There were birds in the sky but I never saw them winging / There was love all around but I never heard it singing." Loesser affectionately called "Till There Was You" Meredith's deaf, dumb, and blind song.

One of my fondest memories of Meredith was watching him at a backer's audition performing "Gary Indiana." It was a soft-shoe charm song he wrote for a lisping child that "hardly hath any etheth in it." "Gary Indiana / Gary Indiana / Let me say it wunth again / If you'd like to have a logical ekthplanathyun / How I happened on thith elegant thinkopathyun / will say without a moment of hethitathyun / There ith jutht one plathe / That can light my fathe." There wasn't a dry angel within spritzing distance from the piano.

# 1958–1959

Broadway Theatre
Opened Thursday, May 21, 1959
David Merrick and Leland Hayward present:

## Gypsy

Book by Arthur Laurents; Suggested by memoirs of Gypsy Rose Lee;
Music by Jule Styne; Lyrics by Stephen Sondheim; Settings and Lighting
by Jo Mielziner; Costumes Designed by Raoul Pene du Bois; Entire Production Directed and Choreographed by Jerome Robbins.
*Cast*: Ethel Merman, Jack Klugman, Sandra Church.

Given the subject matter—the vaudeville/burlesque circuit from the
early twenties to the early thirties—and at Ethel Merman's insistence,
the producers enlisted Jule Styne to compose the music for *Gypsy*, rather
than Sondheim, whom Robbins had suggested. It was an inspired choice.
Styne's flashy showbiz career, his ability to write hit tunes, and his success
with stars Judy Holliday and Carol Channing were reassuring to Merman
after her experience with the unknowns (Matt Duby and Harold Karr)
who had written *Happy Hunting* for her.

Styne and Sondheim kept Merman happy with "Some People" (match-
ing her strident delivery with butts and guts lyrics), "Small World,"
"You'll Never Get Away from Me," and "Everything's Coming Up
Roses," which, as part of an eleven o'clock reprise of "Rose's Turn,"

stunned Broadway audiences with her stammering, touching characterization. Jerome Robbins condensed ten years on the circuit, from Baby June to Dainty June, with a ten second stop-motion lighting effect, and staged "You Gotta Have a Gimmick" as if he worked for Minsky's Burlesque. But the book, music and lyrics were the heart and soul of Gypsy, which remains today one of the greatest Broadway musicals of the past fifty years.

"Let Me Entertain You" lived up to its promise; first as a "school days" clog-step waltz for Baby June and her troupe, then as a raunchy bump-and-grind strip-tease for grown-up sister Louise, also known as Gypsy Rose Lee. Sondheim's perfectly innocent lyrics for Baby June, "Let me entertain you / Let me make you smile / Let me do a few tricks / Some old and then some new tricks / I'm very versatile," take on a whole new meaning when Gypsy Rose Lee sings them while undressing on stage. In hindsight, the collaboration of Styne and Sondheim was evermore remarkable for the harmony of music and lyrics. Inside Steve was a composer dying to get out, yet he let Jule be Jule, and wrote lyrics that seem inevitably wed to Styne's music. "You'll Never Get Away from Me" had another wonderful Styne melody for Merman and a charming duet interlude for Jack Klugman; it was his first musical moment in Gypsy, and Merman nearly slugged him for missing the interjection, "Ah, Rose." The interlude had a range of five notes. No one was taking any chances, and Merman sang rings 'round the counter-melody. As fond as I am of this song, I never quite understood Sondheim's odd turn of phrase: "How you're gon-na not at all / Get away from me." If asked he would probably say, "I like it," and tell me to smoke on my pipe and put that in. The melodies poured out of Styne; "Small World" had an unusual bridge with lots of accidentals, and credit Sondheim for the memorable "We have so much in common / It's a phenomenon." "Mr. Goldstone" was great fun and gave Sondheim the opportunity to use the adjective "peachy" a second time in the same show. Hey, how else would you rhyme lichee? "All I Need Is the Girl" and "Little Lamb" were extravagances heaped on the musical in order to dramatize Louise's hidden feelings about her lack of motherly attention, as well as her dream to dance with Tulsa, the troupe's leading man. The appeal of a dancer selling a number entertained, although we knew it was a stage-wait, but nothing could make us bear the little bear lyric in "Little Lamb."

The triumphant opening trumpet blast of the overture: Ba-ba-ba-Baaa! / Baa-ba-ba-ba-Baaa / Baba!, is a leitmotiv later established in "Some People" ("I had a dream / A wonderful dream / Papa!"), and developed further as an introduction for "Everything's Coming Up Roses." The combination of this repeated theme reaches a climax in "Rose's Turn," a hallucinogenic composite of Rose's past—with musical references from "Some People," "Roses," "You Gotta Get a Gimmick, "Let Me Entertain You," and "Mr. Goldstone"—culminating with: "I dreamed it for you, June / It wasn't for me, Herbie / And if it wasn't for me / Then where would you be / Miss Gypsy Rose Lee?" It doesn't get any better than that.

# 1959–1960

Lunt-Fontaine Theatre
Opened Monday, November 16, 1959
Leland Hayward, Richard Halliday, Richard Rodgers and
Oscar Hammerstein II present:

## The Sound of Music

Book by Howard Lindsay and Russel Crouse; Suggested by *The Trapp
Family Singers* by Maria Augusta Trapp; Music by Richard Rodgers; Lyrics by Oscar Hammerstein II, Directed by Vincent J. Donehue; Musical
Numbers staged by Joe Layton; Scenic Production by Oliver Smith;
Costumes by Lucinda Ballard.
*Cast*: Mary Martin, Theodore Bickel; Kurt Kazner, Patricia Neway.

When *Gypsy*'s Ethel Merman, once again Broadway's top leading lady,
was asked what she thought of Mary Martin's opening night performance
in *The Sound of Music*, she replied: "How can ya knock a nun?" Rodgers
and Hammerstein told us about a Maria of a different kind: "A flibber-
tigibbet / A will o'the wisp! / A clown!" Her Mother Superior muses:
"How do you catch a cloud and pin it down / . . . How do you keep a
wave upon the sand / . . . How do you hold a moon-beam in your hand?"
This is wonderful introspection and brilliant exposition for Maria, the
undisciplined nun, who is destined to fall in love with the father of the
seven children entrusted to her care. When a past Rodgers and Ham-

merstein governess in Siam felt afraid, she whistled a happy tune. Maria does the same . . . well, nearly: "When I'm feeling sad / I simply remember my favorite things / And then I don't feel so bad!" "The Lonely Goatherd" was a rhyming dictionary set to an infectious octave-jumping yodel, and a pastiche German brass band accompaniment. "Do Re Mi," as with "My Favorite Things," celebrated the child in all of us and made it fun to learn the C major scale. To this day I hear students refer to the seventh note on the scale as a drink with jam and bread. "Edelweiss" sang of a bygone Austria, in yet another effortlessly memorable melody from Richard Rodgers. "Climb Ev'ry Mountain" was the obligatory Rodgers and Hammerstein song of inspiration; however, my heart was blessed with the sound of music when I heard, "To sing through the night like a lark who is learning to pray."

The treacle that Rodgers and Hammerstein drained from this sugar-refined story gave them a huge hit that pleased audiences all over the world. It was one of the few musicals that benefited from the film version, due to the exquisite photography of the authentic Austrian countryside, and Julie Andrews, who was the correct age for Maria. It was also the last show Rodgers and Hammerstein would write together; Hammerstein died the following year. "Do Re Mi," "My Favorite Things," and "Climb Ev'ry Mountain" kept the Broadway establishment happy for a few more years, but Elvis was gaining.

---

Broadhurst Theatre
Opened Monday, November 23, 1959
Robert E. Griffith and Harold S. Prince present:

## *Fiorello!*

Book by Jerome Weidman and George Abbott; Music by Jerry Bock; Lyrics by Sheldon Harnick; Choreography by Peter Gennaro; Scenery, Costumes and Lighting by William and Jean Eckart; Directed by George Abbott.
Cast: Tom Bosley, Howard Da Silva, Ellen Hanley, Pat Stanley.

Rodgers and Hammerstein's *The Sound of Music* opened the week before Jerry Bock and Sheldon Harnick's *Fiorello!* In a mere seven days two decades of collaboration ended for one team of writers, and for the other, two decades were about to begin. Jerry and Sheldon started as special material writers, which simply meant they were funny. Bock wrote sketches for Camp Tamiment summer shows, music for Sid Caesar and Max Leibman's television "Admiral Broadway Revue," while Harnick was contributing material to Broadway revues such as *Two's Company, New Faces of 1952,* and *John Murray Anderson's Almanac.* Bock wrote the score (with Holofcener and Weiss) for Mr. *Wonderful,* which produced a terrific song, "Too Close for Comfort"; and Harnick's "The Shape of Things" for *The Littlest Revue* (which Frank Music published) was an early example of his wit, erudition and felicity of phrase. *The Body Beautiful* was their first Broadway show, but it all came together with *Fiorello!*

*Fiorello!* had the exuberance and moxie of its title character, including the exclamation point. H. L. Menken wrote: "Politicians as a class radiate a powerful odor. What really concerns them first, last, and all the time is simply their own jobs." Bock and Harnick's "Politics and Poker" revealed the source of that odor by musicalizing a ward heeler's poker game criteria for selecting a congressman: "How about Dave Zimmerman? / Davy's too bright / . . . How about Frank Monahan? / What about George Gale? / Frank ain't a citizen / And George is in jail / We could run Al Wallinstein / He's only twenty-three / What about Ed Peterson? / You idiot! / That's me!" . . . Politics and poker / Running neck and neck / If politics seems more / predictable that's because usually you can stack the deck!" Jerry Bock's genius for supplying the correctly dramatic music at the right moment set the lyric in waltz tempo to underscore the frivolity of their cynicism. Another waltz, "Till Tomorrow," is more romantic, and like "Tonight," uses Shakespeare's *Romeo and Juliet* as inspiration: "Clouds drifting by / echo a sigh: / Parting is such sweet sorrow." Harnick's knowing lyrics gave the New York City politicians a lovable point of view, and Bock soft-shoed the rogues and charlatans into a "Little Tin Box": "Mister 'X' may we ask you a question? / It's amazing is it not? / That the City pays you slightly less then fifty bucks a week / Yet you've purchased a private yacht? / I am positive your Honor must be joking / Any working man could do what I have done / For a month or two I simply gave up smoking / And put my extra pennies, one by one / Into a little tin box." The politicians are still tap dancing today.

*Fiorello!* won the Pulitzer Prize that year, and I remember promising myself one day I would work with Bock and Harnick.

———————————

Martin Beck Theatre
Opened Thursday, April 14, 1960
Edward Padula in association with L. Slade Brown presents:

# Bye Bye Birdie

Book by Michael Stewart; Music by Charles Strouse, Lyrics by Lee Adams; Scenery by Robert Randolph; Costumes by Miles White; Lighting by Peggy Clark; Directed and Choreographed by Gower Champion. *Cast*: Dick Van Dyke, Chita Rivera, Paul Lynde.

Adler and Ross were the first new kids on the block with *The Pajama Game* and *Damn Yankees*; they were followed by Sondheim with *West Side Story*, Bock and Harnick's *Fiorello!*, and now it was Charles (Buddy) Strouse and Lee Adams' turn with *Bye Bye Birdie*. In the fifties, Green Mansions Hotel was a summer hiatus where fledgling musical theatre writers could create new scores for eager, out of work singers and dancers. (Think Gene Kelly in *Summer Stock*.) Charles Strouse started there—at the same time as Jerry Bock was at Camp Tamiment—after being educated at the Eastman School of Music, then studying with Aaron Copland and Nadia Boulanger. The combination of Strouse's musical erudition and Lee Adams' waspish wit made their Broadway debut a smash hit. The melody for "An English Teacher" was gorgeous and was warmed by Chita Rivera as Rosie, bemoaning her lost opportunity of being an academician's wife. The success of "America," which Chita introduced in *West Side Story*, didn't intimidate Adams and Strouse from writing yet another Hispanic self-ridicule song, "Spanish Rose," with hilarious results: "Americano / Let me give you a piece of advice / To cross Spanish Rose isn't wise [pronounced 'wice'] / Not Danish / Not British / Not Swedish / Not Yiddish / But Spanish Rose!"

Having published Arthur Hamilton's "Cry Me a River" ("Told me love was too plebeian / Told me you were through with me and"), I knew what a good inner rhyme could do for a song; so when Adams and Strouse's "Put on a Happy Face" insisted: "Take off the gloomy mask of tragedy / It's not your style / You'll look so good that you'll be glad ya'de

/ Cided to smile," I wasn't surprised the number spread sunshine all over the place and became a standard. "A Lot of Livin' to Do" was a sexy, driving sybaritic celebration ("There are girls just ripe for some kissin' / And I mean to kiss me a few!") and "Rosie" was the opposite expression of monogamous contentment: "Me and little Rosie / We will be so cozy by a fire built for two / I once heard a poem that goes: / 'A rose is a rose is a rose.' " Utterly charming, and so what if Adams added an 'a' to Gertrude Stein's "Rose is a rose is a rose" quote. As if ballads, tangos, and soft-show numbers weren't enough, Adams and Strouse wrote a Charleston for an adamant, crazed Paul Lynde: "Kids / With their awful clothes and their rock and roll! / Why can't they be like we were / Perfect in every way / What's the matter with kids today?" Nothing; we just wouldn't acknowledge the answer blowin' in the wind.

Bye Bye Birdie was Gower Champion's directorial debut. His energetic, inventive staging of "The Telephone Hour" and "Shriner's Ballet" increased Broadway's appetite for more director-choreographers. The production also introduced bookwriter Michael Stewart, who would collaborate on many future musicals, including Hello Dolly! Ironically, Bye Bye Birdie was a spoof of the Elvis Presley craze, and the establishment loved making fun of rock 'n' roll. Looking back, it might have been more prophetically entitled Bye Bye Broadway.

## OTHER MUSICALS

Other musicals that season included Saratoga, which had a disappointing score by Harold Arlen and Johnny Mercer, and when Howard Keel sang, "Love Is a Game of Poker," Frank Loesser quipped, "And I'm Oskar Homolka." Greenwillow was Loesser's flop; a kinder, gentler, bucolic musical that he lavished with a haunting score. It sang of teakettles, Clegg's old cow and summertime love. The book didn't work and Frank said, "It's the last time I put a pink sequined gown on a girl who hasn't bathed." Also worthy of note was another off-Broadway entry, The Fantasticks, by Tom Jones and Harvey Schmidt. Still playing after thirty-nine years, it is the longest running musical in history. When I first heard "The Holy Man and the New Yorker," an esoteric parable with music performed at a Ben Bagley revue, I couldn't wait to meet these fellow New Yorkers. When I learned that they were from Texas, only recently arrived, my admiration soared. Once ensconced in Greenwich Village, Jones and Schmidt recreated their University of Texas musical, which became the phenomenon The Fantasticks. "Soon It's Gonna Rain" joined the ranks of exalted rain lyric refrains with this felicitous phrase: "Then we'll let it rain / Rain pell-mell." "Try to Remember" had the wisdom of another time and place and the tenderness of a folk melody: "Deep in December it's nice to remember / Without a hurt the heart is hollow." I shared the "Top Ten Young Men of 1960" accolade of the *Holiday* magazine article with Tom Jones, and experiencing Jones and Schmidt's memorable musical that year inspired me to strike out on my own. Happily, both *The Fantasticks* and Ostrow are still running.

# PART II
## 1960–1970

# The Beginning of the End of Camelot: Rock 'n' Roll 'n' Revolution

The decline of Broadway began with the sixties rock 'n' roll revolution: acid rock, country rock, folk rock, jazz rock—reverberating from Krakow to California—emanating from New Orleans dance blues, rockabilly from Memphis, Chicago rhythm and blues, and vocal group rock. Broadway didn't like Elvis; didn't understand Chuck Berry, Little Richard, and Buddy Holly; and ignored the power of the Beatles. What exciting stage musicals might have been written by them! The theatre also failed to attract incipient playwrights such as Larry Kasdan, Steven Bochco, and George Lucas, who might have given us wildly original plays about the big chill of growing up, the law, and the force. Why did Broadway blow it? My guess is that at the time, the establishment was convinced the golden age would last forever, and these strange new writers were a risky investment. Or perhaps it was the fear of collaboration that turned these ingenious voices away from the theatre. After all, they wrote, performed, produced, directed, published, televised, and recorded their own works, and reached a significantly larger audience. Why trust anyone over thirty? Whatever the reasons, in an age when the medium was the message, Broadway was recycling too much of its past to attract their attention, and we lost a generation of creators.

During this tumultuous decade—when the American dream was threatened by nuclear war, the loss of civil rights, assassinations, psychedelic drugs, a hopeless war in Vietnam, and student revolt—it is significant to note that Broadway chose not to dramatize these events or their effect upon our way of life. The sixties brought many theatre songwriters up from the ranks, such as Lee Adams and Charles Strouse, Jerry Herman, Cy Coleman, Lionel Bart, John Kander and Fred Ebb, as well as first-time musical dramatists like Mitch Leigh and Joe Darion, Burt Bacharach and Hal David, Sherman Edwards, Gerome Ragni, and James Rado and Galt MacDermot. Most of them contributed traditional Broadway fare, with the notable exception of Ragni, Rado and MacDermot, the authors of *Hair*, who sensed the revolution and wrote an American tribal love-rock musical.

Throughout my career it was my good fortune to have unique patrons and benefactors. Frank Loesser, Meredith Willson, Goddard Leiberson, Norman Lear, and, during the late sixties, Edgar M. Bronfman, who financed the early stages of *The Apple Tree* and provided all the capitalization for the very risky musical *1776*. Edgar is now the President of the World Jewish Congress, but when I met him he was thought of as "Mr. Sam's boy," a reference to Samuel Bronfman, Edgar's father, who was the founder and owner of Seagrams. I met him at a party Steve and Nan Birmingham gave in honor of the United States Junior Chamber of Commerce Ten Most Outstanding Men of 1960, of whom I was one. Birmingham had written the story for *Holiday* magazine—with photographs by the great Hans Neimuth, who insisted I pose on the roof of our apartment house standing on top of an ornate marble-top ormolu French chest! When I was introduced to Bronfman he asked what had possessed me to do such a risky thing. It may have been the heady atmosphere of the party, or the second Seagrams and soda I was nursing, or just plain hubris, but I began reciting Teddy Roosevelt: "Far better it is to dare mighty things, to win glorious triumphs, even though checkered by failure . . . ," and feeling pretty superior, paused for breath. Bronfman smiled, and to my astonishment concluded the quote: ". . . then to take rank with those poor spirits who neither enjoy much nor suffer much, because they live in the gray twilight that knows not victory nor defeat." "Edgar," I said, in my best Bogart imitation, "this could be the beginning of a beautiful friendship."

# 1960–1961

Majestic Theatre
Opened Saturday, November 3, 1960
Alan Jay Lerner, Frederick Loewe, and Moss Hart present:

## Camelot

Book and Lyrics by Alan Jay Lerner; Music by Frederick Loewe; Staged by Moss Hart; Musical Numbers by Hanya Holm; Scenic Production by Oliver Smith; Costumes designed by Adrian and Tony Duquette; Lighting by Feder. Based on *The Once and Future King* by T. H. White. *Cast:* Julie Andrews, Richard Burton, Roddy McDowall, Robert Goulet.

It is said that *Camelot* killed Moss Hart (he died in 1961) and prompted Frederick Loewe's retirement. The show had its tryout in Toronto, at the O'Keefe Center, and on opening night it took four hours before the curtain, mercifully, came down. Noël Coward, who had attended, said, "It is as long as *Parsifal*, and not as funny." The dream team of *My Fair Lady* (absent its much needed producer Herman Levin), including Lerner and Loewe, Hart, Julie Andrews, etc., set out to prove lightning could strike the same place twice. For insurance they hired Richard Burton, a brilliant actor and a Welshman who could carry a tune. Unfortunately, the only element that struck the same place twice that evening was Abe Feder's lighting.

The score to *Camelot* was not the inspired writing of previous Lerner and Loewe collaborations. (Often, when success is so overwhelming—as

with their *My Fair Lady*—authors attempt to replicate their "sound.")
Nevertheless, it was a charming notion, in the title song, for King Arthur
to decree perfect weather, and it was an easy number for the exclusively
British borderline singers who would play the King: Burton, Richard Harris, and Laurence Harvey. "How to Handle a Woman" had a clever inner
rhyme: "There's a way said the wise old man / A way known by every
woman / Since the whole rigmarole began." However, Lerner's rhetorical
answer, "The way to handle a woman / Is to love her," was less convincing
than the familiar mantra of the 1948 pop hit song, "Nature Boy." "The
greatest thing you'll ever learn / Is just to love and be loved in return."
Om.

Fortunately, gossip of Richard Burton's sexual prowess and Jacqueline
Kennedy's mention of the President's favorite lyric: "In short, there's simply not / A more congenial spot / For happ'ly-ever-aftering than / Here
in Camelot," focused media attention on this clotheshorse musical and
kept it running. The death of President John F. Kennedy three years after
*Camelot* opened shocked the world. His youthfulness, vigor, idealism, and
the personal images that he and his family conveyed to the nation made
his sudden death seem a personal loss to many citizens. It broke our hearts
and ended our belief in the possibility of *Camelot's* happ'ly-ever-aftering.

---

Imperial Theatre
Opened Thursday, April 19, 1961
David Merrick presents:

# *Carnival!*

Book by Michael Stewart; Based on Material by Helen Deutsch; Music
and Lyrics by Bob Merrill; Directed and Choreographed by Gower
Champion; Settings and Lighting by Will Stephen Armstrong; Costumes by Freddy Wittop; Originally based on story "The Seven Souls
of Clement O'Rielly" by Paul Gallico, and filmed as *Lili*.
*Cast*: Anna Maria Alberghetti, Jerry Orbach, James Mitchell.

Notice the billing for present day musicals: the producers outnumber the cast. In 1961 it didn't take a consortium to produce a show; one dedicated, shrewd, former Indian-reservation lawyer, David Merrick, was enough. Merrick was clever enough to put Gower Champion and Mike Stewart back to work immediately after their *Bye Bye Birdie* hit, and cast the moody unknown Jerry Orbach, from *The Fantasticks*, to take the pressure off Anna Maria Alberghetti. She was given the impossible assignment of trying to make us forget Leslie Caron's portrayal of Lili, from the film of the same name. A seemingly meretricious selection of Tin-Pan-Alley songwriter Bob Merrill ("How Much Is That Doggie in the Window?") also proved to be canny artistic judgment. Merrill's Brill Building music-publishing background gave him the training to write simplified hit songs such as "If I Knew You Were Comin' I'd've Baked a Cake" and "Sparrow in the Treetop," but nothing he had previously written prepared us for the masterful character songs he wrote for *Carnival!*

It was said Bob Merrill composed on a toy xylophone. If so, he must have played it better than Red Norvo, because the melody for "Mira" was as technically difficult as it was beautiful. His lyric was equal to the task, first in the verse establishing repetitious naive phrases for a sheltered young girl (Lili) eager to join the carnival troupe, "I came on two buses and a train / Can you imagine that? / Can you imagine that?" followed by a vivid description of the town she's left, "the kind of town where you live in a house 'till the house falls down," leading into the wistful refrain, "What I liked the best in Mira is / Everybody knew my name." Lili was hired in a heartbeat. When she ends up in love with the sad puppeteer, he has conflicting emotions concerning "Her Face": "If in my two hands I could hold her face / While my finger tips / Kiss her eyes and lips / And make them love and light and shine / But that would take two other hands / Not mine!" A bravado finish, but he doth protest too much, we thinks. So does Lili, and they live happily ever after.

## OTHER MUSICALS

The rest of the season included Lucille Ball's *Wildcat*, with "Hey, Look Me Over," which introduced composer Cy Coleman to the street, and Meredith Willson's second Broadway launch, *The Unsinkable Molly Brown*, which was sunk by an unintelligible Tammy Grimes and an inexperienced theatre director, Dore Schary. (Debbie Reynolds' film version of *Molly Brown*'s "I Ain't Down Yet" redeemed the property.) I recall Willson's meeting with aging producer Laurence Langner of The Theatre

Guild; the author and director didn't get along, and Langner lectured Schary and Willson for twenty minutes on the necessity of "listening to each other." After he finished, Meredith articulated his grievances and turned to Langner for solace, only to find him asleep. It was another dramatization of the malaise that would soon erode the Broadway corpus.

# 1961–1962

Forty-Sixth Street Theatre
Opened Saturday, October 14, 1961
Feuer and Martin in association with Frank Productions, Inc., present:

## How to Succeed in Business Without Really Trying

Book by Abe Burrows, Jack Weinstock and Willie Gilbert; Based on Book by Shepherd Mead; Music and Lyrics by Frank Loesser; Choreography by Hugh Lambert; Scenery and Lighting by Robert Randolph; Costumes by Robert Fletcher; Musical Staging by Bob Fosse; Directed by Abe Burrows.
Cast: Robert Morse, Rudy Vallee, Charles Nelson Reilly.

At first, Frank Loesser didn't want to write the score to *How to Succeed in Business Without Really Trying*. "I've done my wise guy show," he told *Guys and Dolls* producers Cy Feuer and Ernie Martin. Frank was wary of "Cy and Ernie" (he said their names sounded like a Japanese good-bye) and now they were urging him to repeat his successful collaboration with Abe Burrows, who was set to write and direct *How to Succeed in Business Without Really Trying*. Loesser thought his next project should be more challenging. "I've never rhymed in Russian; how about a musical Potemkin, and Catherine the Great?" *Pleasures and Palaces* would be written years later and I believe the only reason he ultimately decided to write *How to Succeed* was in order to help Burrows have a much needed hit. It wasn't the first time he put his career on the line for his friend Abe.

Robert Morse was a sensation as J. Pierrepoint Finch, and the production's cartoon-styled satire of the corporate world produced Bob Fosse's comical take on the desperate employees' "Coffee Break." Loesser's shrewd perception of the business world was humorously on target in "The Company Way," an employee's hymn dedicated to playing it safe. In a breezy, conversational, uniquely Loesser duet, Twimble instructs Finch how to survive: "I play it the company way / Wherever the company puts me / There I'll stay / But what is your point of . . . ? / I have no point of view / Supposing the company thinks . . . ? / I think so too!" It can be said that Twimble was the first employee to anticipate the management downsizing of corporate America. "A Secretary Is Not a Toy" will remain frozen in politically correct amber as a reminder of those quaint days when harassment lawsuits came only from the Internal Revenue Service, not the women at the office. Did Loesser have fun with this! "Not a toy to fondle and dandle and playfully handle in search of some puerile joy / Her pad is to write in and not spend the night in / A secretary is not, is definitely not, employed to do a gavotte, or you know what." Despite Bob Fosse's 12/8 dance break, it was written as a waltz dedicated to all of the secretaries whom Frank had adored—from Betty Good to Margie Gans and beyond. Irving Berlin's secretary was Mynna Dryer, and the music publisher, Buddy Morris, was lucky to have Silvia Herscher to look after Jerry Herman, Adams and Strouse, and Cy Coleman. A legion of these dedicated woman ran the business with little thought of breaking through the glass ceiling. Although today's women have joined the CEO ranks, what hasn't changed is the ego of the self-absorbed executive. Male or female, looking into a mirror and singing, "I Believe in You," they imagine themselves as invincible: "You have the cool clear eyes of a seeker of wisdom and truth / Yet there's that upturned chin / And the grin of impetuous youth." It was a self-love song, releasing pent-up chutzpah with religious fervor, and it was to become the theme song for the likes of Carl Icahn, Ivan Boesky, and Michael Milkin.

---

Shubert Theatre, Philadelphia
Opened Monday, February 19, 1962
Stuart Ostrow presents:

# We Take the Town

Book by Felice Bauer and Matt Dubey; Adapted from the screenplay
"Viva Villa!"; Lyrics by Matt Dubey; Music by Harold Karr; Choreography by Donald Saddler; Settings by Peter Larkin; Costumes by Motley;
Lighting by Tharon Musser; Orchestrations by Robert Russell Bennett
and Hershy Kay; Directed by Alex Segal.
*Cast:* Robert Preston, John Cullum, Carmen Alverez, Kathleen Widdoes.

After *How to Succeed,* I left Frank Music to produce my first solo musical, *We Take the Town,* starring Robert Preston as the legendary Pancho Villa. Villa was assassinated in Mexico City in 1923 by his critics, while we were merely slaughtered when we opened in Philadelphia in 1962. A more experienced producer wouldn't have chosen Alex Segal to direct, but Preston insisted on rehearsals beginning in a month's time and I was panicstricken. *We Take the Town,* a musical about the Mexican revolution, was designed by Peter Larkin in earth colors—mostly orange—and I knew I was in trouble when Segal, upon seeing the completed set, screamed: "I told Larkin, I hate orange!" Kermit Bloomgarden, coproducer of *The Music Man,* urged Preston to bolt the show (not his most collegial moment), but Jerry Robbins came to my rescue the day after opening *Oh Dad, Poor Dad;* he loved the show and agreed to replace Segal. Furthermore, my benefactor, Goddard Leiberson, the head of Columbia Records, had invested $350,000 (the entire capitalization) and offered to put up whatever more it cost to get the show to Broadway. As it turned out, Robbins collapsed during rehearsals and I had an ambulance take him back to East 81st Street. (Five years later, Jerry Robbins was to become my theatre conscience, asking me to run his American Theatre Lab, and to negotiate an agreement with all the theatrical unions for the creation of The New York Public Library Lincoln Center Theatre, Tape, and Film Archives, which was made possible with donations from his *Fiddler on the Roof* profits.) That night, I closed the musical and threw a farewell party for the company. The generosity of my colleagues, however, turned what should have been despair into hope. Meredith Willson flew from Los Angeles to Philadelphia and played the score to *Here's Love.* "Your next musical, Stu," he announced in our crowded, flop hotel room. When I returned to New York, the first phone call I received was from Stephen Sondheim, who asked if I would send him the music to "Silverware," a song he admired from my recently aborted production. In addition to making me feel my first producing attempt had some merit, he also invited me to see *A Funny Thing Happened on the Way To the Forum,* which was to open in a few months. It gave me another reason not to give up. And John Shubert, the remaining scion of the family theatre empire, returned my $20,000 deposit for the Broadway Theatre, with this note: "Try again, kid; we need new producers."

A word about the Shuberts—Lee, Sam and J. J., from Jerry Stagg:

> Crude, often vulgar, uneducated, they made a personal monopoly of the theatre, amassing millions upon millions in the process. When the Great Depression erased their corporate empire, they could have retired, individually wealthy and secure. Instead, they came to an inexplicable decision. They determined to keep the theatre alive. They poured their own money onto the gamble. Almost alone the Shuberts kept the marquee lights burning; three stubborn men fought to save the stage. Why? Perhaps because in these men, who could barely read the plays they mounted, there was a passion for the form they never really comprehended. Somehow they reacted to the beauty, the poetry, the art. They may not have understood, but they loved. (in Garraty, 1974)

Today, symptomatic of the theatre's bottom-line mentality, the Shubert empire is run by its former lawyer, who, I can assure you, would not have returned my $20,000 deposit.

Alvin Theatre
Opened Thursday, May 8, 1962
Harold Prince presents:

# A Funny Thing Happened on the Way to the Forum

Book by Burt Shevelove and Larry Gelbart; Based on plays of Plautus;
Music and Lyrics by Stephen Sondheim; Directed by George Abbott;
Choreography and Musical Staging by Jack Cole; Settings and Costumes
by Tony Walton; Lighting by Jean Rosenthal.
*Cast*: Zero Mostel, Jack Gilford, David Burns, Ron Holgate, Raymond
Walburn, Ruth Kobart, John Carradine.

This was the season for long titles and funny musicals. The only short-
ened billing was Harold Prince dropping the S. from his name. *Forum* was
high class burlesque, presided over by a genius clown, Zero Mostel, and
a breathless cast of second bananas who dropped their panting upon each
entrance. The stylized book and score at first confused out-of-town audiences because George Abbott floundered while trying to set the tone
of the farce. It wasn't until Jerome Robbins came in to doctor the show,
and had Sondheim write an opening number, "Comedy Tonight," that
the musical worked. With Sondheim's stately Prologos refrain, contrasted
with Robbins' prosthesis vaudeville staging, you knew you were in good
feet. Although classically trained by Milton Babbit, composer Sondheim
was first and foremost a dramatist, and he made certain his music was
comfortable for the characters and accessible to the audience. "Everybody
Ought To Have a Maid" extolled the virtues of the working woman 200
years before the Christian era. Notice the meticulous selection of the
word "ought," meaning to have or to own, rather than should or must.
"Everybody ought to have a menial / Consistently congenial / Oh! Oh! /
Wouldn't she be delightful / Sweeping out? / Sleeping in?" In A.D. 1961,
the maid would be called a secretary, and you were warned (with a wink)
she was not to be toyed with. Progress?

# 1962–1963

Lunt-Fontanne Theatre
Opened Saturday, November 17, 1962
Feuer and Martin present:

## Little Me

Book by Neil Simon; Based on novel by Patrick Dennis; Lyrics by Carolyn Leigh; Music by Cy Coleman; Musical Numbers and Dances staged by Bob Fosse; Directed by Cy Feuer and Bob Fosse; Scenery and Lighting by Robert Randolph; Costumes by Robert Fletcher.
*Cast*: Sid Caesar, Nancy Andrews, Virginia Martin, Swen Swenson.

Given the success of *Forum* and *How to Succeed*, comedy reigned on Broadway, and this atmosphere encouraged the creation of *Little Me*. When Sid Caesar was television's king of comedy, sketch writers Neil Simon, Mike Stewart, and Larry Gelbart (among others) wrote his gags. So Feuer and Martin reunited Simon with his former boss, and recruited the *How to Succeed* team of Fosse, Randolph, Fletcher, and Virginia Martin to come and re-praise Caesar. Cy Coleman was a trained musician, pianist extraordinary, and a composer in love with jazz riffs and harmonies. (For "Hey Look Me Over" from *Wildcat*, he bounced a standard 4/4 march around the chromatic scale so effectively it sounded like hip Sousa.) His and Carolyn Leigh's *Little Me* assignment was to write songs for Caesar playing seven different characters. Wisely, they let Simon write the jokes for Sid, and gave their pop songs to the featured players. "I've Got Your Number" for Swen Swenson was a sexy syncopated tune destined to be a dance number—after all, this was a Fosse show—and the intense, driving "On the Other Side of the Tracks" for an impoverished Belle Poitrine (Virginia Martin) put Carolyn into play with Broadway's best lyricists: "Gonna sit and fan on my fat divan / While the butler buttles the tea." The one ballad they did write for Caesar, "Real Live Girl," worked well because Sid played it straight, as a shy soldier boy asking for a dance. It fogged up my glasses and buckled my knees. Carolyn Leigh died at fifty-seven, young at heart. Cy Coleman is the Energizer; still going. . . .

---

Imperial Theatre
Opened Sunday, January 6, 1963
David Merrick and Donald Albery present:

## *Oliver!*

Book, Music, and Lyrics by Lionel Bart; Freely adapted from Charles Dickens' *Oliver Twist*; Directed by Peter Coe; Designed by Sean Kenny; Lighting by John Wyckham; Costumes by M. Berman Ltd.
*Cast*: Georgia Brown, Clive Revill.

This glorious transfer from the West End of London was a smash hit on Broadway, and was the first serious challenge to America's leadership of the musical art form. Sean Kenny's ingenious set of interconnecting wooden planks and platforms established a new standard for mobile scenic design, and Georgia Brown's rich, almost masculine voice couldn't mask a broken heart. Of course, having a great Dickens story is a blueprint for success and Lionel Bart & Company didn't let the master down.

Although Bart was a mover and shaker of England's musicals, the only hit he had in the colonies was *Oliver!* The comic Joe E. Lewis said: "You only live once, but if you do it right, once is enough"; the same can be said about a Broadway musical, and Bart's score did it right. "Where Is Love?" repeating the personal pronoun "I" nine times, is sung by a tearful, searching child: "Must I travel far and wide / Till I am beside the someone who / I can mean something to." There wasn't a dry eye in the house. Bart also knew how to write a charm song, and there's none better than "I'd Do Anything," when Nancy and Dodger send up the gentry with an old fashioned gavotte. Bart wrote a Parisian hurdy-gurdy accompaniment for "As Long as He Needs Me," and Georgia Brown seemed more Mistinguett than a cockney bar maid, but her suffering transcended nationalities: "As long as life is long / I'll love him right or wrong." Nancy carried the torch for Bill Sikes in much the same way Fanny Brice did for "My Man," in the *Ziegfeld Follies of 1921*, and Julie did for "Bill" in *Show Boat*. "Consider Yourself" was the fourth hit song from *Oliver!*, and it extended Broadway's love affair with the Brits, which had begun with *My Fair Lady*. The song was an infectious 6/8 march, replete with cockney slang: "Nobody tries to be la-di-dah and uppity / There's a cup of tea / For all." Orphaned Oliver Twist finds a friend in the Artful Dodger, who offers the entreaty every boy longs to hear: "Consider yourself at home / Consider yourself one of the family." Indeed, Lionel Bart's songs for *Oliver!*, like Lerner and Loewe's *My Fair Lady* score for Bernard Shaw's *Pygmalion*, has enhanced the original work. Dickens' Fagin will seem evermore enterprising after listening to "You've Got To Pick a Pocket or Two," and "Food, Glorious Food" will smell better in a theatre than in a book. Another tribute to Bart's talent was the wrath of some Richard Rodgers fans who suggested that Bart had stolen some of Rodgers' melodies.

---

Eugene O'Neill Theatre
Opened April 23, 1963
Harold Prince in association with Lawrence N. Kasha and
Philip C. McKenna present:

## She Loves Me

Book by Joe Masteroff; Based on a play by Miklos Laszlo; Music by Jerry Bock; Lyrics by Sheldon Harnick; Musical Number staged by Carol Haney; Directed by Harold Prince; Setting and Lighting by William and Jean Eckart; Costumes by Patricia Zipprodt.

*Cast*: Barbara Cook, Jack Cassidy, Daniel Massey, Barbara Baxley, Ludwig Donath.

A jewel-box of a musical, filled with precious songs and dazzling performances! Masteroff, Bock and Harnick were on to something new for Broadway—literate, romantic, and without big production numbers—an intimate musical. The choreographer's billing, "Musical *Number* staged by Carol Haney," testified to how little a dance enthusiast could expect. The Eckarts' design was masterful and conjured up the elegance of a tasteful, Austro-Hungarian specialty shop. (Only the device for the passing of seasons—icicles suddenly appearing above Maraczek's window—jarred.) Barbara Cook's "Ice Cream" was a moment I save for a rainy day, and Jack Cassidy found his most memorable career role as Mr. Kodaly, the villain you can't help but love.

We've had many examples of the Soliloquy Song, in which a character, alone on stage, confesses and questions his/her thoughts and feelings, and none is more poignant than "Will He Like Me?" Something bruised inside of Sheldon Harnick enabled him to express Amalia Balash's feelings of insecurity and desperation when she is faced with meeting her "Dear Friend," who until now has been a writing correspondent. "Will he like me? / "Who can say? / How I wish that we could meet another day / It's absurd for me to carry on this way / I'll try not to / Will he like me? / He's just got to." (I'd be surprised if we all didn't feel the same before our first date.) "Days Gone By" was more than nostalgia. Bock and Harnick transform Maraczek into his younger self as he tentatively remembers a melody and a girl who happened to catch his eye, then re-enacts the waltz steps of his life, reaching a vibrant crescendo: "One, two, three / Follow the beat around, around, around / All night / Circling the floor / till dawn lit up the sky / No one younger than I / in days gone by." Ludwig Donath had me dancing again. Auditioning for a sales position in Maraczek's store, Amalia's talent becomes evident when she convinces a chocolate junkie that the shop's music box is her salvation: "When you raise the lid the music plays / Like a disapproving nod / And it sings in your ear / No more candy my dear! / In a way, it's a little like the voice of God." Bock's accompaniment is also heavenly. Georg, the "Dear Friend," is equally nervous and upset at the prospect of meeting his unknown pen pal, and the writers give him a torrent of thoughts in one breath. "Tonight at Eight" requires a singer with world-class lungs: "I'll know when this is done / if something's ended or begun / And if it goes all right, / who knows I might / propose tonight at eight! (Inhale.) The title song, "She

Loves Me," has the syncopated musical drive of Count Basie's Band, including an eleven-beat "Johnny One Note" build at the end of its bridge to galvanize the last chorus; it also displays the exuberant lyricism of Georg's unguarded feelings now that he knows the lady in question is Amalia: "I'm tingling / such delicious tingles / I'm trembling / What the heck does that mean . . . ? / But still I'm incandescent / and like some adolescent / I'd like to scrawl on every wall I see: / She loves me!" I wish I had said that.

# 1963–1964

Sam S. Shubert Theatre
Opened Thursday, October 3, 1963
Stuart Ostrow presents:

## *Here's Love*

Book, Music and Lyrics by Meredith Willson; Book based on "Miracle on 34th Street"; Story by Valentine Davies; Screenplay by George Stevens; Settings by William and Jean Eckart; Costumes by Alvin Colt; Lighting by Tharon Musser; Dances and Musical Numbers staged by Michael Kidd; Directed by Stuart Ostrow.
*Cast*: Janis Paige, Craig Stevens, Laurence Naismith, Fred Gwynne, Paul Reed, David Doyle, Cliff Hall.

Meredith Willson's adaptation of the classic film *Miracle on 34th Street*, re-entitled *Here's Love*, was my first production to reach Broadway. I also replaced Norman Jewison as director, and with the help of Michael Kidd's dances and musical staging, the show was a soft hit. (It recouped its investment.) Janis Paige and television star Craig Stevens were understandably insecure at having a novice director, so I wasn't surprised when, after asking Craig to exit at a certain point, he asked: "How many steps should I take?" or when Janis asked for an entirely new wardrobe during the premiere tryout in Detroit. Comics Fred Gwynne and David Doyle were more tolerant; even I couldn't kill their laughs. Gwynne (who became one of our great character actors), with true show business grit, returned to open the show after the tragic drowning of his baby daughter during rehearsals. My fondest memory of the musical (aside from Meredith's generosity) was the encouragement I received from the gypsy chorus of *Here's Love*. Fixing the show out of town was like a trip to the dentist; so, when after another grueling session with the stars a particularly talented dancer who had watched every rehearsal told me, "It's getting better," I believed him. His name was Michael Bennett. Our smash opening in Washington, D.C., helped boost morale, and allowed the cast and crew a hot August afternoon off to attend Martin Luther King's Freedom March and hear his inspiring "I Have a Dream" speech. The perks of being a pre-Broadway hit were numerous, but none was more special than having Evelyn Lincoln, President Kennedy's secretary, escort my wife around the Oval Office (Ann got to sit in JFK's rocking chair) in return for two house seats to the National Theatre.

---

St. James Theatre
Opened Thursday, January 16, 1964
David Merrick presents:

# *Hello Dolly!*

Book by Michael Stewart; Music and Lyrics by Jerry Herman; Suggested by Thornton Wilder's play *The Matchmaker*; Directed and Choreographed by Gower Champion; Settings by Oliver Smith; Costumes by Freddy Wittop; Lighting by Jean Rosenthal.
*Cast*: Carol Channing, David Burns, Charles Nelson Reilly, Alice Playton.

*Hello Dolly!* was the quintessential Broadway hit; it ran for 2,844 performances. The underpaid clerks of an 1890 misanthropic merchant of Yonkers sneak off to New York to have some fun. There they have various ludicrous adventures as they try to have a good meal, kiss a pretty girl, and hide from the merchant. All ends happily as a result of the machinations of the comical and fun-loving Dolly Levi, a woman who arranges things and ensnares the wealthy merchant for herself. Gower Champion's mastery of the Broadway stop-the-show number was realized with the staging of the title song. Seemingly hundreds of white-aproned waiters line the path for Dolly, as she descends the Tivoli Gardens staircase to the chant of: "Hello, Dolly / Well, Hello Dolly / It's so nice to have you back / Where you belong!" Have we ever been as thrilled during the past thirty-three years? "Hello Dolly" proved to be one of the most (if not the most) popular songs in the canon. With the reluctant help of Louis Armstrong—who didn't want to record it—everyone, upon hearing a plunking banjo, felt the room swayin'. Mack David had written a similar melody for "Sunflower, You're My Sunflower" and he sued Herman; when they settled out of court to avoid a protracted lawsuit, all Mrs. David said to her husband was, "Sunflower, huh?" Then she punched him. Jerry Herman wrote a new number while out of town, "Before the Parade Passes By," for the Act One finale. It was yet another march (the seventh since "Seventy-Six Trombones") and it was an inspiration for Social Security recipients: "Before the parade passes by / I'm gonna go and taste Saturday's high life." Carol Channing at age seventy-eight is still playing Dolly Levi without any sign of just passing by life. "It Only Takes a Moment" was a beautiful ballad delivered by the comic character Cornelius (Charles Nelson Reilly), which reduced its chances for the Hit Parade. Nevertheless it is one of Herman's underrated best: "I held her for an instant / But my arms felt sure and strong / It only takes a moment / To be loved a whole life long."

---

Winter Garden
Opened Thursday, March 26, 1964
Ray Stark presents:

# *Funny Girl*

Book and Story by Isobel Lennart; Music by Jule Styne; Lyrics by Bob Merrill; Directed by Garson Kanin; Musical Numbers staged by Carol Haney; Scenery and Lighting by Robert Randolph; Costumes by Irene Sharaff.

*Cast*: Barbra Streisand, Sydney Chaplin, Kay Medford, Danny Meehan, Jean Stapleton.

"I'm the Greatest Star" introduced the character Fanny Brice in *Funny Girl*, and Barbra Streisand to the world. They were one, inseparable, and the inspiration for this musical. Who else has ever owned the role? "Have you guessed yet who's the best yet?" You, Babs. With the help of Jerome Robbins, who once again was called out of town to save the show, and Styne and Merrill's thrilling score, Barbra was Fanny Brice incarnate. Styne's rhythmically driving refrain for "Don't Rain on My Parade" is matched by Merrill's blizzard of lyrics: "Don't tell me not to live, just sit and putter / Life's candy and the sun's a ball of butter / Who told you you're allowed to rain on my parade?" With "People" and "The Music That Makes Me Dance," Barbra propelled the audience to its feet at a time when you had to earn a standing ovation. Today, audiences applaud when they buy their tickets.

Barbra Streisand first knocked me out in 1961 when she was performing at The Blue Angel, and again when she was auditioning to be cast in *We Take the Town*, opposite Robert Preston. "The part calls for an aristocratic Mexican lady," I said, somewhat apprehensively. "So what," she replied; "When I sing, there is no nationality." I was sold, but Preston wanted an experienced actress and turned me down. (Ironically, she later recorded "How Does the Wine Taste?" from our score, and of course, she was right.)

## OTHER MUSICALS

Like most love affairs, Stephen Sondheim and Arthur Laurents' *Anyone Can Whistle* had good intentions but was out of control. Herbert Ross' direction didn't help, but Lee Remick was radiant, and Angela Lansbury surprised us with her musicality. The title song was a glimpse into Sondheim's soul: "Maybe you could show me how to let go / Lower my guard / Learn to be free / Maybe if you whistle / Whistle for me."

Herbert Greene (at piano), Robert Weede, Frank Loesser, and Jo Sullivan at the first reading of *The Most Happy Fella* in New York, 1956. (Credit Friedman-Abeles)

Cecil Kellaway, Frank Loesser, and Stuart Ostrow at the *Greenwillow* original cast recording in New York, 1960.

Robert Preston as Pancho Villa in *We Take the Town* at the Shubert Theater, Philadelphia, 1962. (Credit Friedman-Abeles)

Laurence Naismith, President Harry S. Truman, Craig Stevens, Janis Paige, and Richard M. Nixon backstage at *Here's Love* at the Shubert Theatre, New York, 1963. (Credit Sam Siegel)

Stuart Ostrow, Meredith Willson, Janis Paige, Laurence Naismith, and Michael Kidd on opening night of *Here's Love* at the Shubert Theatre, 1963. (Credit Sam Siegel)

Sheldon Harnick, Jerome Coopersmith, Jerry Bock and Stuart Ostrow at the backer's audition for *The Apple Tree*, New York, 1966. (Credit Sam Seigel)

Mike Nichols, Alan Alda, Barbara Harris, Earl Wilson, Stuart Ostrow and Robert Alda waiting for opening night reviews of *The Apple Tree* at Sardi's, New York, 1966. (Credit Sam Seigel)

Ron Holgate, Sherman Edwards, Stuart Ostrow, Peter Stone, and Peter Hunt at the Tony Awards Ceremony. 1776 won Best Supporting Actor, Best Musical, and Best Director. New York, 1969.

Stephen Schwartz, Bob Fosse, Roger O. Hirson, and Stuart Ostrow at the first reading of *Pippin* at Broadway Arts, New York, 1972. (Credit Van Williams)

Candy Brown, Ben Vereen, and Pam Sousa in the *Pippin* television commercial, 1973. (Credit Martha Swope)

Stuart Ostrow, David Dukes, B. D. Wong, and John Lithgow, as Dukes replaced Lithgow as Gallimard in M. *Butterfly*, New York, 1988.

# 1964–1965

Imperial Theatre
Opened Thursday, November 22, 1964
Harold Prince presents:

## Fiddler on the Roof

Book by Joseph Stein; Based on Sholom Aleichem's Stories; Music by Jerry Bock; Lyrics by Sheldon Harnick; Directed and Choreographed by Jerome Robbins; Settings by Boris Ahronson; Costumes by Patricia Zipprodt; Lighting by Jean Rosenthal.
Cast: Zero Mostel, Maria Karnilova, Austin Pendleton, Beatrice Arthur.

"Too Jewish," said William Paley, Chairman of the Board of CBS, and also a Jew; so after years of similar rejections, the original producer of *Fiddler on the Roof*, Fred Coe, was compelled to sell the rights to Harold Prince, who ultimately delivered it to Broadway. Jerome Robbins told me it was the memory of his father that inspired him, and the great director nurtured the creative process by constantly insisting the writers answer a crucial dramatic question: "What is it about?" Finally the answer came: Tradition. Wisdom is rare, so when it surfaces in a Broadway musical it is indeed a cause for celebration. *Fiddler on the Roof* is the case in point. Here was the music from the God of Abraham and Isaac, accessible to all religions.

Talking to God ("If I Were a Rich Man"), Tevye muses that although it's no disgrace being poor, it's no great honor either. Bock and Harnick then take the bold step of writing an authentic Yiddish chant as a lilting refrain, ignoring the Broadway establishment naysayers' advice not to be "too Jewish": "Wouldn't have to work hard / Daidle, deedle, diadle, digguh, digguh, deedle, daidle dum / If I were a biddy rich / digguh, digguh, deedle, daidle man." The writers understood that the desire to be rich is universal, whether it's implored by a poor milkman in Anatevka, Russia, or a Lotto player in Anaheim, California. In "Matchmaker," Yente, who schemes to bring about a marriage in an old country 1905 shtetl, has the same assignment as another turn of the century matchmaker, Dolly, from Yonkers. (Coincidentally, *Dolly* and *Fiddler* both opened on Broadway in 1964, across the street from each other.) Tevye's three unmarried daughters, imagining Yente telling them she's found each a match, gaily mimic her pragmatism: "Hodel O Hodel / have I made a match for you! / He's handsome! / He's young! / All right he's sixty-two." Their bravado and self-ridicule turns into halting restraint for the final chorus: "Dear Yente, see that he's gentle / Remember you were also a bride / It's not that I'm sentimental / It's just that I'm terrified!" In this brief moment Bock and Harnick demonstrate Tzeitel, Hodel, and Chava's vulnerability and explain nineteenth-century marriage traditions. In a more contemplative waltz, Bock and Harnick's ceremonial prayer for "Sunrise, Sunset" cries out to parents of the bride and groom throughout the world. "What words of wisdom can I give them? / How can I help to ease their way? / Now they must learn from one another / Day by day." "Miracle of Miracles" was somehow overshadowed by the rest of this landmark score—possibly due to its being performed by a comic character—but miraculous nevertheless. With Old Testament references, a timid tailor celebrates his marriage to the woman of his dreams: "Wonder of wonders / miracle of miracles / God took a Daniel once again / stood by his side and, / miracle of miracles / walked him through the lion's den." Having a sagacious comedy number in the second act of a musical is valuable because it provides welcome relief from the plot. Rarely does it dramatize character, as it does for Tevye and Golde in "Do You Love Me?" "Do I love him? / For twenty-five years I've lived with him / fought with him, starved with him. / Twenty-five years my bed is his / If that's not love, what is? / Then you love me? / I suppose I do / And I suppose I love you too." Is it any wonder that *Fiddler on the Roof* is performed in countries worldwide? You don't have to be Jewish to take love for granted. Zero Mostel was brilliant as Tevye, the milkman, but he became so unpredictable—ad libbing lines and screaming at the other actors on stage—that Prince didn't renew his contract. Hal was right, and *Fiddler on the Roof* proved to be more than a Zero.

## OTHER MUSICALS

Two musicals in particular stand out. The first, *Golden Boy*, was in many ways a groundbreaking event: The artful projections of lighting designer Richard Pilbrow, the inspired direction of Peter Coe (who was wrongfully replaced by Arthur Penn), and the best score Adams and Strouse would write illuminated and updated the Clifford Odets play. The 1937 brash young Italian-American prizefighter, Morris Carnovsky, was now a struggling ghetto boxer, Sammy Davis, Jr. Adams and Strouse were stretching themselves in 1964 with "I Want to Be with You," a tender aria for Davis to sing to his intended white bride: "Tonight I'm touching you holding you, world you're gonna see / We'll make out some how! / Here's my girl and me! / You can't hurt us now!" Thrilling, and impossible. "Don't Forget 127th Street," "Lorna's Here," and "This Is the Life," along with Jamie Rogers' fight choreography, had audiences cheering during its Philadelphia tryout. If only the producer had left well enough alone, *Golden Boy* "coulda bin" a contender.

The other musical, *The Roar of the Greasepaint and the Smell of the Crowd*, brought back Anthony Newley (of *Stop the World I Want To Get Off* fame) with another hit song, "Who Can I Turn To When Nobody Needs Me?" British star Cyril Ritchard was at his music hall best, and numbers staged by Gillian Lynne (who would choreograph *Cats* eighteen years later) were as clever as Sean Kenny's rocky place setting. "On a Wonderful Day Like Today" was in keeping with Broadway's Pollyanna view of the times, yet the world was not always wonderful. On August 11, 1965, thirty-five people were killed and hundreds injured during riots in Watts, Los Angeles, that were set off when a white policeman stopped a black driver. About $200 million in property was burned, looted, or destroyed. A far cry from "On a morning like this I could kiss everybody / I'm so full of love and good will / For the world's in a wonderful way / On a wonderful day like today."

# 1965–1966

Anta Washington Square Theatre
Opened Monday, November 22, 1965
Albert W. Seldon and Hal James present:

## Man of La Mancha

Musical Play by Dale Wasserman; Book and Musical Staging by Albert
Marre; Music by Mitch Leigh; Lyrics by Joe Darion; Choreography by
Jack Cole; Settings and Lighting by Howard Bay; Costumes by Howard
Bay and Patton Cambell.
*Cast*: Richard Kiley, Joan Diener, Irving Jacobson, Ray Middleton, Rob-
ert Rounsville.

*Man of La Mancha* forged a new route to Broadway, via the Goodspeed
Opera House in East Haddam, Connecticut; the same theatre would originate *Annie* twelve years later. It opened in a makeshift off-Broadway
house built to house the new Lincoln Center Repertory Company. The
rampway, no-frills ANTA (American National Theatre and Academy)
space was a perfect setting for this risky show, emphasizing its seriousness
of purpose. Suggested by the life and works of Miguel de Cervantes y
Saavedra, all the characters in the musical are imprisoned in a dungeon
in Seville at the end of the sixteenth century, and the entire musical
takes place there and in various other places in Cervantes' imagination.
Howard Bay's ingenious set and costumes and Jack Cole's choreography—

notably masked dancers representing horses (which *Equus*, in 1973, would imitate) and the rape of Aldonza—elevated Marre's staging to thrilling heights. Richard Kiley's mesmeric performance as Don Quixote was never more moving as when seven dancers holding mirrored shields confront him with the reality of his age and bewildered condition. The score, by Mitch Leigh and Joe Darion, matched the aspirations of Dale Wasserman's intelligent book. The Spanish Pasodoble is a dance in quick 2/4 time, but Leigh and Darion placed their title song, "Man of La Mancha (I, Don Quixote)" in 3/4 time with thrilling results. Leigh's jingle writer background didn't prepare Broadway for his depth of talent as a composer (he studied at Yale with Paul Hindermith); his vigorous rhythmic choices, along with Darion's orthodox "thou" and "whither" lyrics, made you believe that an impoverished gentleman in an old suit of mail, upon a bony nag, was the dauntless knight known as Don Quixote de la Mancha.

Cervantes wrote of Don Quixote: "It seemed unto him very requisite and behooveful . . . that he himself should become a knight-errant, and go throughout the world . . . to seek adventures, and practice in person all that he had read was used by knights of yore; revenging all kinds of injuries, and offering himself to occasions and dangers, which being once happily achieved, might gain him eternal renown." Writing a song to match Cervantes was a formidable challenge but happily proved to be a textbook lesson on how to distill the essence of a character, as exemplified by their "The Impossible Dream (The Quest)." We hear Quixote's credo set as Ravel-inspired bolero: "To dream the impossible dream / To fight the unbeatable foe / To bear with unbearable sorrow / To run where the brave dare not go / . . . And the world will be better for this / That one man scorned and covered with scars / Still strove with his last ounce of courage / To reach the unreachable stars!" *Man of La Mancha* did.

Palace Theatre
Opened Saturday, January 29, 1966
Fryer, Carr and Harris present:

# *Sweet Charity*

Book by Neil Simon; Music by Cy Coleman; Lyrics by Dorothy Fields;
Based on film *Nights of Cabiria* by Federico Fellini; Staged and Choreographed by Bob Fosse; Scenery and Lighting by Robert Randolph; Costumes by Irene Sharaff.
*Cast*: Gwen Verdon, John McMartin, Helen Gallager, Thelma Oliver.

Here was Bob Fosse at his full-fledged director-choreographer best with
Gwen Verdon again, this time with a wonderful score by Cy Coleman
and Dorothy Fields. "Bumps," "Hits," and "Catches" are burlesque terms
referring to a trap-drummer's accentuated beats for a stripper's sleazy
dance step, pelvic grind, and breast-tasseled-twirl, and a musical was
never more sexually explicit than in Coleman and Fields' opening number
for *Sweet Charity*, "Big Spender." Taxi-dancers at a seedy dance hall size
up their prospective "Johns" by singing a syncopated come-on, swollen
with phallic references, then breathe heavily and simulate a climax: "Do
you wanna have (*Bump*) fun (*Bump*) fun? / How about a few (*Hit*) laughs
(*Hit*) laughs? / I can show you a (*Catch, Catch*) good time / Hey Big
Spender! / HEY BIG SPENDER!! / . . . ssspend a little time with me."
"There's Gotta Be Something Better" is a wanting song, in the tradition
of "Somebody, Somewhere," and "Corner of the Sky," but with a difference. Rather than one person's pensive soliloquy, it is sung and danced
by three floozies who want to get out of "The Life." The heavily accented
jazz-waltz tempo is exuberant, and Nickie, Helene, and Charity's deter-
mination is as infectious as it is admirable. "There's gotta be some re-
spectable trade / There's gotta be something easy to learn / And when I
find me something easy to learn / I'm gonna get up / I'm gonna get out /
I'm gonna get up get out and / Learn it!" Dorothy Fields' sympathy for
shady ladies (such as Cissy in *A Tree Grows in Brooklyn*) captures our
hearts once again. She understood that the underdog always has the edge

in musicals, and you care when Charity, in a poignant lament, asks, "Where Am I Going?" Coleman and Fields could also be playful about adversity, as in "If My Friends Could See Me Now," when Charity, on one of her tricks, winds up in a film star's sumptuous apartment and celebrates her good fortune with a Jimmy Durante strut: "All I can say is wow-ee look-a / Where I am / Tonight I landed Pow! / Right in a pot of jam / What I set-up / Holy cow! / They'd never believe it / If my friends could see me now!"

*Sweet Charity* was a hit and Fosse was asked to direct the movie, starring Shirley MacLaine. In certain ways the film was better. Ben Vereen, Paula Kelly, and Chita Rivera were cast, and because Bob started in films as a dancer (*Kiss Me Kate*, *Dobie Gillis*), his knowledge of camera angles and set-ups gave the film authentic theatrical energy.

---

Winter Garden Theatre
Opened Tuesday, May 24, 1966
Fryer, Carr and Harris present:

# *Mame*

Book by Jerome Lawrence and Robert E. Lee; Based on the novel *Auntie Mame* by Patrick Dennis, and play by Laurence and Lee; Music and Lyrics by Jerry Herman; Directed by Gene Saks; Dances and Musical Numbers staged by Onna White; Settings by William and Jean Eckart; Costumes by Robert Mackintosh; Lighting by Tharon Musser.
*Cast:* Angela Lansbury, Beatrice Arthur, Jane Connell.

*Mame* was another Patrick Dennis adaptation (*Little Me* was the first), a record for Broadway source material, and another star turn. Equally lovable and excessive, Mame was cloned from Dolly by Jerry Herman. In a shameless evocation of his previous hit, *Hello Dolly!*, Herman got his banjos strummin' and plunkin' out a tune to beat the band for *Mame*. What separated the one title song from the other was a *glissando*. "You coax the blues right out of the horn / *Mame* / You charm the husk right off'a the corn / *Mame*," and instead of waiters, this Southern Dolly had a chorus of men in red fox-hunt attire singing her praises. Once more, the power of a hit song was enough to sustain this old-fashioned show. Angela Lansbury, primarily known as a dramatic actress, was able to transform the sentimentality of the story into a touching musical ("If He Walked into My Life"), and in a Crosby-Hope comedy number with her friendly enemy ("Bosom Buddies"), she proved she could slug it out with the best: "If I say that your tongue is vicious / If I call you uncouth / It's simply that / Who else but a bosom buddy / Will sit down and tell you the truth?" Of course it didn't hurt having Bea Arthur around to spar with. Blame Jerry Herman for rushing the Christmas season with "We Need a Little Christmas." The song has become a seasonal standard (encouraged in great part by retail stores) but its value for *Mame* was its last sixteen bars, which helped to establish the character: "For I've grown a little leaner / Grown a little colder / Grown a little sadder / Grown a little older / And I need a little angel / Sitting on my shoulder / Need a little Christmas now!" Notice how often show tunes end with the word *now* followed by an exclamation point. Why? Musical theatre is action and energy at the moment it is uttered, propelling the character to move the story.

## OTHER MUSICALS

*Pickwick*, an English import, had tenor Harry Secombe at the top of his tessitura with "If I Ruled the World," and *On a Clear Day You Can See Forever* teamed Alan Jay Lerner with Burton Lane. The title song, along with "Come Back To Me," survived a week production. Barbara Harris was a convincing actress, but not up to the demands of the music. (It took another Barbra—Streisand—to star in the film and memorialize the score.) When a psychiatrist loses his susceptible student patient in an extrasensory perception episode, "Come Back to Me" restores her to reality, and Alan Jay Lerner to Broadway lyric luster: "Hear my voice where you are / Take a train; steal a car / Hop a freight; grab a star / Come back to me! / In a Rolls or a van / Wrapped in mink or Saran / Anyway that you can / Come back to me!" Alan, you were great on a clear day.

# 1966–1967

Shubert Theatre
Opened Thursday, October 18, 1966
Stuart Ostrow presents:

## *The Apple Tree*

Music by Jerry Bock; Lyrics by Sheldon Harnick; Based on stories by
Mark Twain, Frank R. Stockton, and Jules Feiffer; Book by Jerry Bock
and Sheldon Harnick; Additional Book material by Jerome Cooper-
smith; Directed by Mike Nichols; Additional Musical Staging by Her-
bert Ross; Choreography by Lee Theodore; Production and Costume
Design by Tony Walton; Lighting by Jean Rosenthal; Animation Film
Sequence by Richard Williams; Hairstyles by Ernest Adler.
*Cast*: Barbara Harris, Alan Alda, Larry Blyden.

After writing *Fiddler on the Roof*, Jerry Bock and Sheldon Harnick were
studying the short story form as the basis for their next musical when I
called and asked if they would be interested in creating an evening of
three musicals connected to a common theme. (Television had reduced
the audience's attention span to half hour programming—why not try it
on stage?) Our original title was *Come Back, Go Away, I Love You*, and
it became *The Apple Tree* after Mike Nichols agreed to direct his first
musical, starring Barbara Harris and Alan Alda. In the beginning we tried
casting Al Freeman, Jr., an African American, as Adam, but we got cold

feet; then we tried an unknown, Dustin Hoffman, who couldn't sing (Nichols would remember Hoffman for *The Graduate*), but it was Alda's audition of "If I Only Had A Brain" that won him the role.

The first song Jerry and Sheldon wrote for "The Diary of Adam and Eve" portion of the evening was "Beautiful, Beautiful World," an opening number expressing Eve's first awareness of the beauty around her. It was a diversified, curious, fascinating, bountiful, beautiful, beautiful song; when it became obvious during rehearsals that Barbara Harris couldn't sing it, we all felt prematurely expelled from the Garden of Eden. God created heaven and earth in six days; it took Bock and Harnick five to create a replacement opening number, "Here in Eden," another miracle, albeit a professional one: "It's all so lovely / I may just weep / I love this garden and everything that's in it / And something tells me to treasure every minute / Blossom and bud / Mountain and mud / I know I'll be happy / Perfectly happy / Here in Eden." Everything happens for the best. Writing the world's first love song for Adam to sing about Eve is as difficult as trying to bottle a kiss. Nevertheless, the writers met the dramatic challenge by having Adam irritated with Eve: "She keeps filling up the hut with rubbish / Like flowers and plants / And not only is it overcrowded / It's loaded with ants." Bock and Harnick change the mood in the release, from a measured drone to a freewheeling burst of melody and astonished revelation: "Once I saw her standing on a hill-top / Her head tilted back / The sunlight on her face / Gazing at the flight of a bird / And suddenly I saw that she was / Beautiful / Beautiful, yes, that's the word." "What Makes Me Love Him" in other hands could have resulted in a song wallowing in sentimentality. Not so with the authors of *The Apple Tree*: "What makes me love him / It's quite beyond me / It must be something I can't define / Unless it's merely that he's masculine / And that he's mine." After the first twenty-five years of creation, it's nice to know.

Tony Walton was our brilliant designer and was overwhelmed by having to design both scenery and costumes for three musicals at the same time. During rehearsals I received an emergency call from the scenery shop to look at the set being built for Act One, "The Diary of Adam and Eve." What I saw was a disaster. Tony had designed an Eden stamped out of plastic molds where everything—the shelter, trees, lakes, and animals—was translucent! It looked like *Star Wars*, not Mark Twain. When I confronted Mike Nichols with the colossal problem of lighting such surfaces, he merely said (in his best Caligula imitation): "It's what I want. If you desire genius, you must pay for it," and threatened to walk. Walton agreed there was a problem but he felt a loyalty to deliver Nichols' vision, so I paid for it—$80,000 of trouble. When we had our technical rehearsal in Boston, it took Jean Rosenthal four days (unheard of in 1966) to light plastic city, but now we were finally ready to run the show. "Barbara, Alan, on stage!" Nichols called out. "We're here," two disembodied voices replied. *We couldn't see the actors!* Nichols turned pale, then said to me, "Tell Tony it doesn't work; throw it out, we need another set." Walton was inconsolable. He knew the cost of the set was a third of the show's budget, and like the snake in Eden, I didn't have a pit to hiss in. But it was spring, and when I saw Tony sketching under a tree in the Boston Gardens, I was hopeful the new set would be closer to nature. It was; organic, beautiful, and down to earth at $9,000.

What do Robert Klein, Herbert Ross and Nora Kaye, Jerome Robbins, Jacqueline Kennedy, Lillian Hellman, Mia Farrow, Gloria Steinem, Penelope Gilliatt, Richard Williams, Alexander Cohen, and Warren Beatty have to do with *The Apple Tree?* Answer: Klein was in the chorus—his first Broadway show—direct from Chicago's *Second City.* Directors/choreographers Herb and Nora commuted from Hollywood to help their friend Nichols, who was a terrific comedy director but froze every time the music started. Jerome Robbins, our original director (don't ask), came to our rescue during previews in New York and unified the three stories by having the Narrator wear a tuxedo in each act. President Kennedy's widow, Hellman, Farrow, Steinem, and Gillatt were Nichols' personal friends who showed up during Hollywood pre-production conferences, New York rehearsals, and the Boston tryout. (I nearly swooned when Mrs. Kennedy tapped me on the shoulder and asked how much I was paying the musicians.) Richard Williams (the genius film animator who later did *Who Framed Roger Rabbit?*) created a stunning five-minute montage for the transformation of Barbara Harris' Ella to Passionella. Warren Beatty was dating Barbara when she was nominated for the Best Musical Actress Tony Award and was scheduled to appear on producer Alex Cohen's first nationally televised Tony Awards program. The afternoon of the telecast Alex called me and said: "You'd better come to the theatre, Stuart, Barbara doesn't want to come out of her dressing room." When I arrived Barbara addressed me as Nichols: "Mike, Please tell Stuart I'm sorry but I can't go on," and walked out the stage door. I followed her on to a downtown bus, and then to her town house on Fifth Street in Greenwich Village. Her friends tried to help me coax her back uptown, but she was clearly not herself. It wasn't until I called Beatty that I discovered they had just split up. Miraculously he got her to the theatre, through the awards performance and ceremony (she won) and even brought her to the gala party afterward. Where she still called me Mike.

———————

Broadhurst Theatre
Opened Sunday, November 20, 1966
Harold Prince in association with Ruth Mitchell presents:

# *Cabaret*

Book by Joe Masteroff; Based on play *I Am a Camera* by John Van Druten and stories by Christopher Isherwood; Music by John Kander; Lyrics by Fred Ebb; Directed by Harold Prince; Dances and Cabaret Numbers by Ronald Field; Scenery by Boris Aronson; Costumes by Patricia Zipprodt; Lighting by Jean Rosenthal.
*Cast:* Joel Grey, Bert Convey, Lotte Lenya, Jack Gilford, Jill Haworth.

There were so many musicals in the fifties and sixties that an aspiring musical dramatist could learn how to develop his craft in much the same way as apprentice artists did in the Renaissance by grounding colors, priming wooden panels, making brushes of hog's hair, and learning technical skills such as casting and soldering. Adler and Ross, Bock and Harnick, Adams and Strouse, and Kander and Ebb all learned their craft by coaching singers and writing dance arrangements, pop songs, and revue material before collaborating on Broadway. This apprentice-master system all but disappeared in the seventies because fewer new musicals were being produced.

The first time I heard Fred Ebb audition a score was for a musical he wrote with Paul Kline in the late fifties called *Morning Sun*, and I recall a shy, rather nervous man who delivered an intensely emotional performance. I had the same experience listening to the audition of *Cabaret* when I was a member of the Theatre Guild Subscription Committee. Fred is one of those songwriters who can wring the tears out and play naughty with a lyric; he is so good that performers mimic his style. Composer John Kander set Fred's *Cabaret* lyrics perfectly and together they established the team's métier: nightclub acts, roller rinks, burlesque, vaudeville, dance marathons—in essence, showbiz. *Cabaret* had the musical echo of Kurt Weill and the look of George Grosz's depraved Berlin, replete with prostitutes, fat Junkers, smug bourgeoisie, sottish drinkers, lechers, and hypocrites. "Willkommen," the musical's opening number, set the period and style of the show brilliantly, and Boris Aronson's nightclub set of distorted (mylar) mirrors established the danger and decadence of pre-war Nazi Germany. It was such a powerful moment that the rest of the show never worked as well outside the cabaret atmosphere. The sinister M.C. of the Kit Kat Klub set the decadent tone of 1930s cabaret by dancing and romancing an onstage mock gorilla with "If You Could See Her." In the song's coda, reminding us of the period, farce turns to terror when he tells us: "I understand your objection / I grant you my problem's not small / But if you could see her through my eyes / She doesn't look Jewish at all." "Tomorrow Belongs To Me" was another sobering reflection of what the Nazis had in store for the world. The song is a combination of hymn ("Deutschland Uber Alles") and Goethe nature poem; an Aryan youth begins the insistent refrain, which is repeated by his countrymen with such force that we are compelled to see, hear, and almost smell the evil.

The show version interlude to the title song, "Cabaret," is the essence of the number. Speaking of her friend Elsie, Sally Bowles explains: "The day she died the people came to snicker / Well that's what comes from too much pills and liquor / But when I saw her laid out like a Queen / She was the happiest corpse I'd ever seen." Then came the famous chorus: "Life is a cabaret, old chum / Come to the cabaret." It was an instant hit, momentarily liberating America from its anti–Vietnam War demonstrations and Black Power threats, and celebrating Timothy Leary's dictum: turn on, tune in, drop out.

*Cabaret* was Harold Prince's best directorial job to date, but it was overshadowed by Bob Fosse's movie version starring Liza Minelli, both of whom owed their Broadway debuts to Prince. The only thing wrong with this wonderful production was it beat out *The Apple Tree* for the season's Best Musical Tony Award.

# 1967–1968

Biltmore Theatre
Opened Monday, April 29, 1968
Michael Butler presents the Natoma Production of:

## *Hair*

Book and Lyrics by Gerome Ragni and James Rado; Music by Galt
MacDermot; Directed by Tom O'Horgan; Dances Directed by Julie
Arenal; Costumes by Nancy Potts; Scenery by Robin Wagner; Lighting
by Jules Fisher.
*Cast*: Gerome Ragni, James Rado, Lamont Washington, Lynn Kellogg.

The supporting cast of the sixties landmark musical *West Side Story*
introduced a new generation of performers and creators. The chorus line
of *Hair*, the American Tribal Love-Rock Musical, included Melba Moore,
Shelley Plimpton, Paul Jabara, and Diane Keaton among its alumni.
When I first saw it (at music publisher Nat Shapiro's invitation) I thought
I was visiting another planet. The poetry, morals, and thwarted aspirations of the flower-children counter-culture era found their voice in this
second generation landmark musical of the decade. The Biltmore Theatre
smelled of pot and the onstage rock band inspired dancing in the aisles
and frontal nudity from the performers.

The musical was an outgrowth of the anti–Vietnam War, drug culture
scene; its score, especially "Let the Sunshine In," spoke in hallucinogenic

tongues. Thank Canadian composer Galt MacDermot for making musical sense of it, with an inspired refrain repeated ad infinitum. This pioneer rock musical also offered a mystic song inspired by the eleventh Zodiacal constellation, "Aquarius," and once again MacDermot's melody—this one a middle eastern Arabian-nights chant—made it an international hit. *Hair* was a rock concert dressed up (or down, if you consider the nude first act finale) to be a musical. The story was almost nonexistent, but witnessing these hippie flower-children on a legitimate stage brought a new generation of theatregoers to Broadway. It was a sensation that promised a new direction for Broadway. Not surprisingly, the wise guys hated it and gave the Tony Award for Best Musical that year to my production of *1776*. Plus ça change, plus c'est la même chose. It's taken thirty years, a moribund musical theatre, and the AIDS plague for the landmark musical of the nineties, *Rent*, to break through and interest a new audience.

# 1968–1969

Sam S. Shubert Theatre
Opened Sunday, December 1, 1968
David Merrick presents:

## Promises, Promises

Book by Neil Simon; Based on screenplay "The Apartment" by Billy
Wilder and I. L. Diamond; Music by Burt Bacharach; Lyrics by Hal
David; Directed by Robert Moore; Musical Numbers staged by Michael
Bennett; Settings by Robin Wagner; Costumes by Donald Brooks;
Lighting by Martin Aronstein.
*Cast*: Jerry Orbach, Jill O'Hara, Marion Mercer.

David Merrick, producer of *Promises, Promises*, understood Broadway
needed more hit songs and hired pop songwriters Burt Bacharach and Hal
David ("What the World Needs Now," "The Look of Love," "Do You
Know the Way to San Jose") to hype his new musical. They didn't let
Merrick down; they wrote "I'll Never Fall in Love Again," delivering yet
another Dionne Warwick smash recording. Bacharach was a skilled musician and his sense of harmony and rhythm was unique. The quirky
signature moment of "I'll Never" occurs at the end of its refrain, when
the tempo switches from 4/4 time to 2/4, then back to 4/4. Unlike Merrick's other Brill Building import, Bob Merrill, Bacharach and David
didn't make the transition from popular music to musical theatre, either

due to a lack of interest or because they won the Academy Award the next year for "Raindrops Keep Falling on My Head" and consequently were offered film musicals to write, such as *Lost Horizon*.

The greatest question musical dramatists must answer is: does the story I am telling sing? Is the subject sufficiently off the ground to compel the heightened emotion of bursting into song? Will a song add a deeper understanding of character or situation? For *Guys and Dolls*, the authors musicalized a short story by Damon Runyon ("The Idyll of Sarah Brown") into a full length theatre classic. E. B. White once said, "Plays come about as close to literature as a problem in solid geometry." That may be so, but true literature has been a great resource for theatre. Consider this list of musicals adapted from books: *A Tree Grows in Brooklyn* by Betty Smith; *Anna and the King of Siam* by Margaret Landen; *My Sister Eileen* by Ruth McKenney; *7½ Cents* by Richard Bissell; *The Year the Yankees Lost the Pennant* by Douglas Wallop; *Candide* by Voltaire; *Memoirs of Gypsy Rose Lee* by Ms. Lee; and *The Trapp Family Singers* by Maria Augusta Trapp; *The Once and Future King* by T. H. White; *How To Succeed in Business Without Really Trying* by Shepherd Mead; *Little Me* by Patrick Dennis; *Don Quixote de la Mancha* by Cervantes; *The Diary of Adam and Eve* by Mark Twain; *The Lady or the Tiger?* by Frank Stockton; and *Passionella* by Jules Feiffer. Since the mid-century more than half of the musicals included in this book have found their origins in literature. Musicals adapted from plays have also succeeded: *Kismet* by Edward Knoblock; *The Beggar's Opera* by John Gay; *Pygmalion* by George Bernard Shaw; *They Knew What They Wanted* by Sidney Howard; *Romeo and Juliet* by Shakespeare; *The Plays of Plautus*; *The Shop Around the Corner* by Miklos Laszlo; *The Matchmaker* by Thornton Wilder; and *I Am a Camera* by John Van Druten.

What hasn't worked as well is the concept of adapting a film to the stage. Garbo's *Ninotchka* was far superior to Cole Porter's *Silk Stockings*, as was the film *Lili* to *Carnival! Promises, Promises* suffers the same fate, possibly because the stage cast couldn't compete with the memorable film performances of Jack Lemmon and Shirley MacLaine in *The Apartment*, but primarily, I think, because screenplays are merely blueprints for the director, cinematographer, and film editor to shoot reels of reality, close-ups, and point-of-view reactions to tell a story. Once these images are reflected on the screen, the remaining dialogue is merely a representation of the story. Theatre requires conflict, character, and catharsis; that begins and ends with words, not pictures.

# 1776

Forty-Sixth Street Theatre
Opened Sunday, March 16, 1969
Stuart Ostrow presents:

Music and Lyrics by Sherman Edwards; Book by Peter Stone; Based on a conception of Sherman Edwards; Scenery and Lighting by Jo Mielziner; Costumes by Patricia Zipprodt; Directed by Peter Hunt; Musical Numbers staged by Onna White.
*Cast*: William Daniels, Howard DaSilva, Ken Howard, Betty Buckley, Paul Hecht.

*1776* was the musical no one wanted to produce. Sherman Edwards, a former schoolteacher, offered it around Broadway for eleven years; Sheldon Harnick asked me to listen to it after collaborating with me on *The Apple Tree*. I had known Sherman from my Frank Music Corp. publishing days but was unaware of his passion for American history until I heard his opening number, "Sit Down, John."

Great opening numbers can work wonders for a musical by setting the tone, style, authenticity, and level of entertainment. "Comedy Tonight" informs us the show is a farce, "Fugue for Tinhorns," a fable, and "Tradition," a folk tale. In "Sit Down, John," a cranky John Adams, Massachusetts Member of the Second Continental Congress in Philadelphia, 1776, is singing: "I say vote yes! / Vote for Independency!" while being exhorted by Members of the other twelve states to shut up! "It's ninety degrees! / Have mercy, John, please / It's hot as hell in / Philadelphia!" Magically, we know within twelve bars what to expect for the rest of the evening. I loved the score to *1776*, but the odds of raising money in 1968 for a musical comedy about the signing of the Declaration of Independence were as unfavorable as betting in 1775 that England's King George III would give up his American colonies. Furthermore, Edwards' book wandered and it wasn't until Peter Stone agreed to dramatize the musical along the lines of *Twelve Angry Men* did I feel we had a shot to be fired around the world. When Stone agreed to rewrite Edwards' book, one of the brilliant changes he made was to introduce John Adams to the audience in front of the curtain, before we hear a note of music:

> *John Adams*: I have come to the conclusion that one useless man is called a disgrace, that two are called a law firm, and that three or more become a congress. And by God, I have had this Congress!

He continues, giving us the time, place, temperament, and mission of the musical; when the curtain flies it reveals the Continental Congress in session, sweltering in the heat of a premature summer's evening, and shouting Adams down in ever-expanding harmony: "John, you're a bore! / We've heard this before! / Now for God's sake / John / Sit down!" Sherman Edwards had the inspiration, and Peter Stone increased the aggravation.

The heroes of our *1776* were portrayed as fallible, lusty, obnoxious, disliked, foolish, prejudiced, and altogether human. This sacrilegious dramatization of America's demigods sent historians into shock and theatre audiences into gales of delighted laughter. No example was more ridiculous, nor as vain, as the musical's Richard Henry Lee; in a sprightly canter, "The Lees of Old Virginia," he proposes his state, Virginia, is to be the Mother of American Independence: "And may my horses turn to glue / If I can't deliver up to you / A resolution on independency!" To complete the cartoon, Edwards gives Lee an "Old Macdonald's Farm" ride-off: "Here a Lee! There a Lee / And I'll come back / Triumphant-Lee / Forr-warr / Ho-ooo!" It stopped the show, set the irreverent tone, and prompted an encore (and a Tony Award) for Ron Holgate.

The problem of making John ("obnoxious and disliked") Adams likable was solved by Stone and Edwards' seamless collaboration of scene and song. Recalling his letters to wife Abigail, Adams meets her in certain reaches of his mind and expresses his innermost feelings. Peter Stone is the sole bookwriter in the canon who can write dialogue exchanges as if they were lyrics:

> *John*: Oh, Abigail—I'm very lonely, Abigail.
>
> *Abigail*: Are you, John? Then as long as you were sending for wives, why didn't you send for your own?
>
> *John*: Don't be unreasonable, Abigail.
>
> *Abigail*: Now I'm unreasonable—you must add that to your list.

*John:* List?

*Abigail:* The catalogue of my faults you included in your last letter.

*John:* They were fondly intended, Madame!

*Abigail:* That I play at cards badly?

*John:* A compliment!

*Abigail:* That my posture is crooked?

*John:* An endearment!

*Abigail:* That I read, write, and think too much?

*John:* An irony!

*Abigail:* That I am *pigeon-toed?*

*John:* Ah, well, there you have me, Abby—I'm afraid you *are* pigeon-toed. (Smiling) Come to Philadelphia, Abigail, please come.

You couldn't ask for a more authentic song cue, and the duet that followed ("Yours, Yours, Yours") was also deceptively formal, yet heartfelt and sensual: "Come soon as you can to my cloister / I've forgotten the feel of your hand / Soon Madame we shall walk again in Cupid's grove together / And we'll fondly survey that promised land!"

"Momma, Look Sharp" gave Edwards the opportunity to write an authentic folk lament for a dying soldier; rather than indulge in fancy staging, Peter Hunt, our director, simply put the actor in spotlight and let him sing. With each decision we made to pare down *1776*—especially confining most events to the chamber of the Continental Congress—the musical improved. (Howard DaSilva quit out of town when we cut Benjamin Franklin's vulgar frolic, "Doozie Lamb," sung in a New Brunswick whorehouse, but returned after seeing his understudy, Rex Everhart, get even more laughs without the song.) Edwards wrote two strong melodies for "Momma, Look Sharp"; the first was a 32 bar refrain for a dying soldier crying out for his mother, and the second was her reply in the bridge of the song. Then in a stunning moment when we return to the refrain, we realize the soldier is delirious and it is he who is singing his mother's comforting lyric, preparing himself to die. It is as powerful an antiwar sentiment as I have ever heard.

We had trouble casting a ladylike Martha Jefferson; I thought we had hit bottom when the unknown Betty Buckley, looking like a cheerleader and straight off the plane from Texas, began her audition by saying, "Howdy!" "You're very pretty, Miss Buckley, but not the type; thank you," I said. "Won't y'all least hear me sing?" replied a future Norma

Desmond, and before I could say no, she was into "Johnny One Note," and she performed it magnificently. I turned to Peter and Sherman and asked: "If you were Thomas Jefferson and hadn't seen your wife for six months, wouldn't you finish writing the Declaration of Independence the minute Betty Buckley walked in the door?" And that is exactly how Peter Stone rewrote the scene.

One hundred ninety-two years later, America was again experiencing troubled times. In 1968 dissent and doubt regarding the war in Vietnam tore at the Republic, and the country was shocked by the assassination of Martin Luther King, Jr., and Senator Robert F. Kennedy, and by violence surrounding the party conventions in Miami and Chicago. The reason I thought that producing *1776* was so timely was its relevance to the protest to end the war in Vietnam. America was thwarting Vietnam's revolution in much the same way England sought to defeat us in 1776. It was my secret, and ironically, after President Richard M. Nixon invited us to perform at the White House, the nation's right wing conservatives lauded the musical's patriotism. No one ever knew, however, that at the eleventh hour a tough lady on Nixon's staff called me with a list of songs the White House insisted be cut from the show for the President's guests. She demanded we take out "Cool, Cool, Conservative Men," "Momma, Look Sharp," and "Molasses To Rum." (The three were anti-conservative, anti-war, and anti-race hypocrisy, respectively.) I refused, and it was William Safire, former flack for the League of New York Theatres, then a speech writer for President Nixon, who convinced the White House to have *1776* performed in its entirety. The only other occasion the prestigious East Room was ever so humbled was when Abigail Adams used it to hang out the family laundry.

## OTHER MUSICALS

The only other musical of quality this season was *Zorba*, with a score by Kander and Ebb, directed by Hal Prince, and designed by Boris Aronson and Richard Pilbrow. The shaft lighting of a Bouzouki circle made an indelible impression, as did the show's opening number, "Life Is," and the widow, Carmen Alvarez.

# 1969–1970

Alvin Theatre
Opened Sunday, April 26, 1970
Harold Prince in association with Ruth Mitchell presents:

## Company

Music and Lyrics by Stephen Sondheim; Book by George Furth; Directed by Harold Prince; Sets and Projections by Boris Aronson; Costumes by D. D. Ryan; Lighting by Robert Ornbo; Musical Numbers staged by Michael Bennett.
*Cast*: Dean Jones, Elaine Stritch, Charles Kimbrough, Jon Cunningham, Donna McKechnie, Susan Browning, Beth Howland.

*Company* was a brilliant collaboration, and the first one between director Prince, Sondheim, and choreographer Michael Bennett. Boris Aronson created an environment of levels and projections reflecting Manhattan living and Sondheim looked through a glass darkly at the morals and mores of his generation.

The last thing you'd expect in a Sondheim tract on marriage is a square dance hoe-down gliss ("Uh-huh / Mm-hm"), but it is precisely the contrast needed in his musically sophisticated "Little Things" and it is what makes it a joy. It was a condemnation of agitated matrimonial life, ironically expressed in rhyme (we do, pursue, accrue, misconstrue, share, swear, wear), which culminates with a very personal Sondheim zinger:

"The concerts you enjoy together / Neighbors you annoy together / Children you destroy together." Uh-huh. "You Could Drive a Person Crazy" is a girl trio parody of a Helen Kane "Boop-boop-a-doo" vocal lick, and Sondheim's unrequited ladies in the lurch don't aspire to anything higher than telling bachelor Bobby off. Here Steve demonstrates he can subordinate Porter: "When a person's personality is personable / He shouldn't ought-a sit like a lump / It's harder than a matador coercin' a bull / To try to get you off-a your rump." Funny and fine. One image I have of Steve Sondheim in the seventies was seeing him biking the midtown Manhattan streets—just another anonymous New Yorker. Perhaps he was writing "Another Hundred People." His intimate knowledge of big city life was fertile ground for mining gems of commentary regarding anonymity, romance, and friendship, and he expresses them as vaudeville turns for the supporting characters in *Company*. "Side by Side by Side" is the cynical version of "Together, Wherever We Go." Hidden in its friendly music-hall sentimentality, Bobby's five married friends ignore their unhappiness and define the musical's title: "One's impossible, two is dreary / Three is company / Safe and cheery." To be certain we got the point, Steve wrote an extended tag for the cast to dance in a frenzied showbiz finale, celebrating its vacuousness. "The Ladies Who Lunch" is the perfect character song; it is written as if it was a one act Chekhov play, where everything about the situation and the lonely person singing is tragically revealed. Only one other song of this caliber, "One for My Baby" by Harold Arlen and Johnny Mercer (curiously, also about a drinker), reveals as much pathos. Elaine Stritch created Joanne, and it's unlikely the song will ever be performed as well. Joanne begins by proposing a raunchy rubato toast, followed by a lazy Bossa Nova beat as she raises her whisky glass and sings: "I'll drink to that." And she does, and does again, attempting to drown her feelings, only to have them rise and shatter the surface. In an inspired last chorus, Joanne exhorts the audience to pay tribute to the seeds of destruction within themselves: "Let's hear it for the ladies who lunch / Everybody rise! / Rise! / Rise!" It was a chilling, confusing moment when we all rose in tribute to the performer (or perhaps to identify with the song's implication), and an unparalleled theatrical accomplishment by Sondheim and Stritch.

## OTHER MUSICALS

*Purlie*, based on Ossie Davis' play, was jazzed up for Broadway and introduced Melba ("I Got Love") Moore and Cleavon Little. *Minnie's*

*Boys* had Lewis J. Stadlen, but even he couldn't overcome a banal score. The same can be said regarding Lauren Bacall's *Applause*. Also doomed was Katharine Hepburn's *Coco*, notwithstanding Michael Bennett's attempt to create musical excitement for what was basically an imitation fashion show.

# PART III
## 1970–1980

# The British Are Coming:
# Andrew Lloyd Webber

Although there were significant home-grown musicals added to the Broadway canon in the seventies, albeit fewer than in previous decades, British composer Andrew Lloyd Webber (now, Lord Lloyd Webber) opened and closed the decade with two of the most original and highly successful ones, *Jesus Christ Superstar* and *Evita*. Webber, recognizing the monopoly Americans had on Broadway and being the first new generation English composer in two decades (following Sandy Wilson and Lionel Bart), greatly enhanced his passport to The Great White Way by choosing American directors (Tom O'Horgan and Harold Prince) to debut his works. If you can't lick 'em, join 'em.

The other calculated dominance in the seventies was the self-empowered Shubert Foundation lawyers' successful displacement of Laurence Shubert Laurence as the last family member to run the dynasty; they crowned themselves heads of the theater chain. Their reign has lasted for nearly three decades, during which time the amount of new musicals produced for Broadway has been drastically reduced. Coincidence? I think not. As landlords, they succeeded in changing the terms of a producer's theatre rental contract, in demanding a larger share of the proceeds, and in many cases, in insisting on being a co-producer. If you can't join 'em, enjoin 'em. The Shubert Foundation prospered, and the ranks of the independent producers thinned. The producer's trade organization, the League of New York Theaters, was no help, as it was run by the Shubert lawyers who heretofore were responsible as paid attorneys for management-labor negotiations and pension and welfare union trusts. Now they ran both ends. As heads of the Shubert Organization they were management. As lawyers, they also represented the union employees. This duality gave them the unprecedented power to orchestrate management-labor contract negotiations and insure there was no chance of a strike on Broadway. (A strike would result in a substantial loss of income, should they be compelled to close any number of their seventeen theatres for the duration). In the past, the Shubert family had joined producers by taking a strike and demonstrating a common will to hold runaway union wage and work demands to a fair minimum; as a result, the cost of producing Broadway musicals remained fairly constant. The turning point came in a 1975 contract dispute with the musicians' union, when Local 802 was offered a huge thirty percent wage increase after threatening to shut Broadway down. At the time, I was receiving substantial royalties and profits from both *Pippin* and *Chicago*; nevertheless, I announced my opposition to the precedent-setting capitulation. I cautioned that if we caved in to the musicians' demand, all the other trade unions would most certainly ask for the same raise (they did) and the cost of producing a Broadway musical would skyrocket (it did). Underestimating the lawyer-landlord's influence over my colleagues, I was quickly humbled when Hal Prince told me he would support my motion to accept the strike, then voted instead to accept the theatre owner's recommendation. The next week I resigned as a member of the League's Board of Governors and as a Trustee of the Musician's Pension and Welfare Fund. I produced *Pippin* in 1972 for $500,000. I was recently offered a budget of $10 million to produce the Broadway revival.

Sensing the disappearance of the independent producer, the Nederlander real estate family began building and buying up more Manhattan theatres, and they became the second largest landlord-producer in New York. Jimmy and Joey Nederlander, however, were the good guys, and they harbored no pretensions to inspire, nurture, develop, or edit the creation of a new musical; that was the producer's job. But faced with keeping their theatres lit, they gambled on what the Shuberts left behind: notably, *Annie* and *Sweeney Todd*. There was still some hope left for the future of the Broadway musical, but now, in order to be a player, you needed more than a plank and a passion.

# 1970–1971

Winter Garden
Opened Sunday, April 4, 1971
Harold Prince in association with Ruth Mitchell presents:

## *Follies*

Book by James Goldman; Music and Lyrics by Stephen Sondheim; Directed by Harold Prince and Michael Bennett; Scenic Production by Boris Aronson; Costumes by Florence Klotz; Lighting by Tharon Musser.
*Cast*: Dorothy Collins, Alexis Smith, Gene Nelson, Yvonne DeCarlo, John McMartin.

While Sondheim was writing *Company*, he was also working with James Goldman and me on another original musical entitled *The Girls Upstairs*, a story about a reunion of Ziegfeld Follies chorines. I was about to produce the musical but withdrew for personal reasons, and Harold Prince agreed to take over after he and Sondheim opened *Company*. It was one of those decisions that changed all our lives.

One of *Follies'* flashback moments at the reunion of the Weismann Follies (read Ziegfeld) was that of Buddy and Ben reliving a particular memory of their chorus-girl dating days, "Waiting for the Girls Upstairs." Combining ghostly musical references with rhythmic exultation, Sondheim captured the innocence, glamour and romance of a bygone backstage life. *Follies* cost a bundle, and every penny of it was on stage. Florence Klotz's divine costumes, Boris Aronson's artistic ruin of a set, and Michael Bennett's ghost-like statuesque Ziegfeld beauties gave the musical a shadowy dimension. Having attended an authentic Ziegfeld Follies reunion, I was struck by the zealotry of its alumni, so I was not surprised to witness 67-year-old Ethel Shutta bring the house down with "Broadway Baby": "Some day, maybe / All my dreams will be repaid / Hell, I'd even play the maid to be in a show!" At that moment Shutta was Sophie Tucker, Nora Bayes, Fanny Brice, and Helen Morgan in one; we cheered the irony of her wish being fulfilled on the stage of the Winter Garden Theater. The durability of these Follies Girls was never more strenuously tested than in "I'm Still Here," written for a now-faded movie star, Carlotta Campion (a clue), and played by faded movie star Yvonne De Carlo. Life imitating artifice. Goldman and Sondheim's device of establishing character by writing pastiches of nostalgic star-turn theatre songs (advanced five years later by the authors of *Chicago*) was effectively realized in "Beautiful Girls" and "Who's That Woman?" but not in "I'm Still Here." Perhaps it was the confusion of Carlotta's film references that made the song feel out of place; nevertheless, no one noticed so long as she was ballsy. For her big finish, not unlike Joanne in *Company*, Carlotta exhorts the audience to applause with: "And I'm here / Look who's here! / I'm still here!" Steal from the best, I say.

*Follies* became a cult classic and the musical won all the awards, yet it never recouped its investment, a symptom of Sondheim shows. (Right or wrong, the litmus test for success on Broadway has always been a show's ability to repay its investors.) Stephen Sondheim attracted a new, more esoteric musical theatre audience: enlightened, cultured, alienated, cynical, but hardly ever joyous, perhaps reflecting the times. Nor were they the vast middle class, who since the thirties had supported Broadway's carefree fare. (I recall Steve admonishing me that the hallmark of Broadway was mediocrity.) For the next twenty-five years Broadway scores would be compared to the cerebral excellence of Sondheim and new writers would attempt to clone his style. Had there been an equally gifted new composer-lyricist working to satisfy the broader emotional needs of an increasingly estranged Broadway audience, perhaps the musical today would be healthier. Unfortunately, the symptom became the disease.

St. James Theatre
Opened Thursday, May 6, 1971
Stuart Ostrow presents:

# Scratch

By Archibald MacLeish; Suggested by Stephen Vincent Benet's short story "The Devil and Daniel Webster"; Directed by Peter H. Hunt; Scenery by John Conklin; Costumes by Patricia Zipprodt; Lighting by Feder.
Cast: Patrick Magee, Will Geer, Roy Poole.

Eager to move on after departing *The Girls Upstairs*, I commissioned Archibald MacLeish and Bob Dylan to write a new musical, *Scratch*. Here's the story I promised MacLeish I would tell one day.

Bob Dylan whined a couplet at me to quit pushing him one afternoon while working in my Pound Ridge studio; something like, "If it comes it comes, if it won't it won't, if it rhymes it rhymes, if don't it don't." Too bad it wasn't a finished song for *Scratch*, the ballad musical I was producing for Broadway. My plan was for MacLeish, the Republic's poet laureate, and Dylan, America's balladeer, to musicalize Stephen Vincent Benet's "The Devil and Daniel Webster," and we were into our third month of unproductive meetings. "How's this?" he asked, handing me a verse and chorus scrawled on a foolscap pad. It was illegible. "Sing it to me, Bob; I can't read Sanskrit," I replied, trying for a laugh and hoping to get him to use the guitar he brought each week, yet never played. Dylan mumbled something, then picked up his guitar and strummed "Father of Night." Finally, a breakthrough! Dylan had translated MacLeish's draft of a scene with Daniel Webster and his client, Jabez Stone, into a duet; a repentant prayer for Stone and a defiant challenge for Webster. The musical was going to work, and musical theatre would hear a new generation's voice.

During the following weeks he finished several songs, including the opening number for *Scratch*, "New Morning." There were other signs of progress: Dylan agreed to meet with director Peter Hunt and Archibald MacLeish in Conway, Massachusetts, and he brought his musical director,

Al Kooper, to Pound Ridge to check me out. It was strange enough driving four hours with Bob Dylan to Conway without him saying a word, but it was nothing compared to the seven hours that followed. The MacLeishes' house was a charming eighteenth-century saltbox, with a woodshed that boasted vintage-scented oak, pine, and copper beech logs for the fireplace. Into this harmony of past and perfect I brought America's troubadour, and he freaked. Peter Hunt, the MacLeishes and I spent the afternoon watching Dylan drink the house brandy as quickly as MacLeish could refill his snifter. He never once responded to any question, or joined the conversation regarding the musical's dramatic problems, but kept belting the bottle down, so by the time we reached Act Two, he was asleep. We were dumfounded. It was time to leave and the only impression the celebrated folk singer had made was a nasty ring from his brandy snifter on the MacLeishes' 1785 cherry table. I've never understood why Bob Dylan froze in front of Archibald MacLeish. Was it awe, or boredom? Whatever, it was a serious warning that I blithely ignored.

It was a grim ride until we reached my home, when Bob asked if he could stay for dinner. After eating, unexpectedly, he sang for his supper by performing all his golden oldies and delighted us further by singing a duet ("Skeeball") with our eleven-year-old daughter. Looking back, I believe it was his way of tipping us. It was a joyous occasion, and the last time I ever saw Bob Dylan. I tried reaching him for weeks, with no success. Was he ill? Did he have another motorcycle accident? MacLeish was in Antigua, attempting to complete his adaptation without Dylan's score, and Peter Hunt and I were deep into the set design. I had raised all the money, the theatre was booked, and we were poised to begin casting the moment Dylan showed up, when Clive Davis, then President of Columbia Records (and the man who introduced us), called: "Stu, Bob's first album since 'Nashville Skyline' three years ago is on release tomorrow and it's a bitch; thanks, pal." Album? Bitch? Pal?

What MacLeish and I hoped for was a seamless collaboration: two American poets dramatizing folklore with song. It was a risky idea from the start, but when Bob Dylan betrayed us, 79-year-old Archibald MacLeish was devastated. Although I knew better, I produced *Scratch* as a play to repay MacLeish for his trust in me. "New Morning," an album by Bob Dylan, Columbia Records #PC30290, was released December 17, 1970. *Scratch*, a play by Archibald MacLeish, opened on Broadway on Thursday, May 6, 1971, and closed May 8, 1971. Requiescat in pace, Archie.

# 1971–1972

Mark Hellinger Theatre

Opened Tuesday, October 12, 1971

Robert Stigwood in association with MCA Inc. by arrangement with David Land presents:

## *Jesus Christ Superstar*

Lyrics by Tim Rice; Music by Andrew Lloyd Webber; Conceived for the stage and directed by Tom O'Horgan; Scenery by Robin Wagner; Costumes by Randy Batrcelo; Lighting by Jules Fisher; Sound by Abe Jacob.
*Cast*: Ben Vereen, Jeff Fenholt, Yvonne Elliman.

Oh shit, Jesus Christ. Please, no irreverence intended; merely an example of contrasting the holy with the prosaic. Tim Rice and Andrew Lloyd Webber's rock opera, *Jesus Christ Superstar*, engaged Christianity in much the same style as their title song. The song had all of Webber's liturgical acumen but it was the chorus' provocative repetition of the Divinely Sent Savior of the World's name, comparing him to a superstar, that caught the public's attention. "Jesus Christ superstar / Do you think you're what they say you are?" A more reverential treatment of Christ was expressed by the musical's Mary Magdalene in "I Don't Know How to Love Him." This tender musical litany by Webber and soul-searching lyric from Rice distinguished the show from those critics who thought it profane by reassuring the audience of the author's religious faith.

Three credits—for lyrics, music, and sound—in the billing heralded a new era; Andrew Lloyd Webber and Tim Rice, who changed the form of the musical, now worked with a sound designer, which signified the end of live on-stage sound. Since the album of *Jesus Christ Superstar* was a smash hit before the stage musical was produced, naturally the theatre had to replicate the recorded sound. Furthermore, the show had a knowing producer, Robert Stigwood, who began his career with Brian Epstein (manager of the Beatles) and understood the value of records to presell an attraction. The album sold millions of copies and audiences came in humming the tunes before the curtain went up. Tom O'Horgan's staging on Robin Wagner's awesome set (the deck rose eighty-five degrees to envelop the actors) was as spectacular as the biblical parting of the Red Sea. Ben Vereen caught everybody's attention, especially mine, and I cast him in my next show, *Pippin*.

Once again however, the establishment ignored the power of something revolutionary, and gave the Tony Award to a musical version of *Two Gentlemen of Verona*.

---

Broadhurst Theatre
Opened Wednesday, June 7, 1972
Kenneth Waissman and Maxine Fox in association with
Anthony D'Amato present:

# Grease

Book, Music and Lyrics by Jim Jacobs and Warren Casey; Directed by Tom Moore; Musical Numbers and Dances staged by Patricia Birch; Scenery by Douglas W. Schmidt; Costumes by Carrie F. Robbins; Lighting by Carl Eigsti; Sound by Jack Shearing.
*Cast*: Barry Bostwick, Carole Demas, Adrienne Barbeau, Walter Bobbie.

A decade after *Bye Bye Birdie*, youth was onstage again with *Grease*; it was not so much a rock'n'roll parody as an homage to the style of the generation's acolytes and priests: Frankie Avalon, Fabian, and of course, Elvis. It began in Chicago as an amateur show and zhoot-doo-wah-wahed its way to New York, where it ran for 3,388 performances. Tom Moore's and Pat Birch's oily ducktails, wraparound dark glasses, electric guitars, and whirlwind dances found their most appreciative audience among those who battled through the confusion of adolescence during the middle and late fifties. Having just turned 40, and knowing there was life after high school, I felt disqualified to judge the kidding vein of "It's Raining on Prom Night," with its glitzy violin chords and fading harp arpeggios, but I did manage a smile for "Beauty School Dropout," and the poor girl who had to slink back to high school because she "flunked shampoo."

Asiatic flu, Sandra Dee, patent leather shoes, taffeta skirts, and virgin pins; loud songs with a heavy beat, and lyrics lost beneath the endless repetition of choral "oo-waddy, oo-waddy, ooooo. . . ." You had to be there.

# 1972–1973

Imperial Theatre
Opened Monday, October 23, 1972
Stuart Ostrow presents:

## *Pippin*

Book by Roger O. Hirson; Music and Lyrics by Stephen Schwartz; Directed and Choreographed by Bob Fosse; Scenery by Tony Walton; Costumes by Patricia Zipprodt; Lighting by Jules Fisher.
*Cast*: Ben Vereen, John Rubinstein, Leland Palmer, Irene Ryan, Jill Clayburgh, Eric Berry.

In spite of, or perhaps because of, my failure to deliver Bob Dylan, I was even more determined to produce a contemporary musical that would appeal to a new generation of theatregoers. Stephen Schwartz, a recent graduate of Carnegie-Mellon University, came to my Broadway office to play the score to *Pippin*. From the moment he played "Corner of the Sky" I knew Stephen was the new voice I was looking for. The rest of the score was just as fresh and when he told me it was Carole King who most influenced his music, I felt the earth move under my feet and agreed to produce it on the spot. Stephen had written *Pippin* as a CMU project (along with *Godspell*, which was about to open off-Broadway) and his book was a college jape. Roger O. Hirson (*World War 2 ½*) had agreed to rewrite the text, and the three of us spent the next year trying to make it work.

It wasn't until Bob Fosse said he would direct that the tone of the musical changed—from a sincere, naive, morality play to an anachronistic, cynical burlesque. The turning point came when Stephen wrote "Magic to Do" and we decided to create a character called the Leading Player (Fosse had Ben Vereen in mind) to narrate and manipulate *Pippin*. Anything to do with magic fascinated Stephen (he would later write a score for *The Magic Show*) and he responded immediately to my suggestion by writing a new opening number over the weekend. A bluesy, mysterious vamp introduced the song, inspiring Tony Walton to design a light curtain where all you could see were disembodied hands and Ben Vereen's face, followed by a hip rhythmic chorus with playful eighth-century lyric references. It foreshadowed the events of the evening (a la "Comedy Tonight"), cleverly balancing the Leading Player's Master of Ceremonies showbiz savvy with Holy Roman Empire asides.

Another crucial moment during the pre-production gestation was when Schwartz and Fosse argued over choosing singers rather than dancers for the chorus. It was a culmination of the many changes of style Fosse had introduced, and it was the first test of authority for an author vis-à-vis his director. I supported Fosse's concept of a dance show and the rupture between them never healed. (Schwartz has never accepted the Broadway version as his own—or ever returned any royalties.)

In exchange for my agreement, *Pippin* would be the first commercial production at the recently completed Kennedy Center Opera House; Roger Stevens invested $100,000 in the production, and I raised the balance of the capitalization from Motown Records, which was accomplished with the crucial guarantee of a Michael Jackson recording of "Corner of the Sky." When the record was released Stephen was outraged because Jackson had changed the lyric to "children *sit in the show*." The song, however, became a smash hit, bolstering our advance box office sales. It was indicative of Stephen Schwartz's character to be steadfast in his authorship, and although we opened in Washington, D.C., to rave notices, he thought his CMU baby was being perverted into a Broadway whore. (Much to his credit, he continued to write the new songs I asked for, such as "On the Right Track" and "Love Song.") The Kennedy Center opening was auspicious and we knew it from the first laugh John Rubinstein got when he appeared in a side theatre box before the curtain rise, asking the pit conductor where the stage was. (The bit was dropped in New York.) I cannot emphasize enough the effect of the first five minutes of a musical. If the initial tune, tone, touch, and tempo of events entertains enough, the show can coast for the next twenty minutes of necessary exposition. But after that, you'd better have another showstopper! Conceived in Sophie Tucker's half-talking style, "No Time at All" did exactly that. It was due in part to Bob Fosse's "follow-the-bouncing-ball effect" and Irene ("Beverly Hillbillies") Ryan's outrageous mugging, but mostly because Stephen wrote an infectious tune and a humorous take on growing old. Furthermore, Schwartz cleverly kept Berthe, Charlemagne's aging mother, in character despite her ribald jests. Carole King's influence on Stephen Schwartz was never more honestly realized than in his rhythmically complicated, yet oddly flowing soft rock "Love Song," which was written to make the relationship between Pippin and Catherine plausible. It was a tricky duet to perform and it added to Jill Clayburgh's dilemma as to whether or not to quit the musical. (Jill was an insecure singer and I'll always be grateful that the song, and John Rubinstein, gave her the confidence to stay.) Bob Fosse never trusted the *Pippin* writing, which is why he staged the show as circus, ballet, musical comedy, minstrel show, rock concert, magic, and vaudeville spectacle. With "Corner of the Sky," however, he knew the song evoked a yearning for fulfillment with the yuppie audiences and had a million dollar refrain, so he didn't try to fix it. He merely put Pippin in a spotlight and let him soar.

Bob Fosse was at war with himself. After completing the brilliant movie of *Cabaret* and a startling television special with Liza Minelli, *Liza with a "Z,"* he was into three packs of Camels a day, pills to help him sleep, pills to wake him up ("It's Showtime!"), booze, broads, and other stimulants not yet known to civilians. Bob was self destructing, burning himself out in order to resurrect a phoenix. During our Washington, D.C., tryout he came to me for solace, and I've never forgiven myself for my reply: "Just keep on doing what you're doing, Bobby; we're going to be a hit!" Ugh. Work was the ultimate narcotic, and the more Fosse force-vomited before rehearsals the more the creativity flowed, so to speak. (He once told me he could fix his life if he rehearsed it long enough.) In the course of rehearsals at the Kennedy Center, Roger Stevens called in terror to tell me to get the company out of the theatre because there was a bomb threat! I ran from the Watergate Hotel to the Opera House and found the company and Fosse deep into a new ten-minute dance for the finale of the show. So as not to panic the cast, I whispered in Bob's ear that we had to evacuate the building immediately; "A bomb is about to go off!" Fosse nodded, turned to the company and told them to run through it one more time. (The dumbest part of this story is I stayed to watch the number.) Leaving Washington for New York was just as bizarre. A death threat was made on Fosse's life by a jealous boyfriend of one of the *Pippin* chorus girls, and I had to ask my connection at the White House to have the secret service escort us to the D.C. city limits. During previews at the Imperial Theatre, I hired two off-duty NYPD officers to guard the rehearsals, until a smart detective told me that Fosse and the chorus girl were getting their kicks out of all the attention, and the way to stop the nonsense was to fire the girl. I did, and she returned the next day—with a black eye from her boyfriend, his honor apparently satisfied—and the threat was withdrawn.

*Pippin* was irreverent, funny, hip, and sexy; a take-off on a young man's search for fulfillment; a parody of war, parents, Crusades, old age, monogamy, religion, and suicide. It was the right show for the seventies and ran for five years; in 1977, it became the tenth-longest running musical of all time.

---

Sam S. Shubert Theatre
Opened Sunday, February 25, 1973
Harold Prince in association with Ruth Mitchell presents:

# A Little Night Music

Book by Hugh Wheeler; Suggested by Ingmar Bergman's film *Smiles of a Summer Night*; Music and Lyrics by Stephen Sondheim; Directed by Harold Prince; Choreography by Patricia Birch; Scenery by Boris Aronson; Costumes by Florence Klotz; Lighting by Tharon Musser.
*Cast*: Glynis Johns, Len Cariou, Hermione Gingold, Patricia Elliot, Laurence Guittard.

There is a trenchant passage in "Liaisons" from *A Little Night Music*, which could easily represent Stephen Sondheim's questioning creed: "Where is style? / Where is skill? / Where is fore-thought? / Where's discretion of the heart, Where's passion in the art, Where's craft?" Of course, he is the preeminent musical theatre practitioner of these virtues.

"A Weekend in the Country" was craft personified, and passion in the art was never more artfully realized than in "Send in the Clowns." Alternating the accompaniment to give proper weight to the thoughts between pauses, Sondheim hides a woman's pain in metaphor when Desiree, Fredrik's former mistress, realizes he no longer wants her. It is quite different from what Canio in the opera *Pagliacci* sings in a wild outburst of grief, bewailing the duel role he is forced to play as a lover and a clown, but equally tragic.

# 1975–1976

Forty-Sixth Street Theatre
Opened Tuesday, June 1, 1975
Robert Fryer and James Cresson present:

## *Chicago*

Book by Fred Ebb and Bob Fosse; Music by John Kander; Lyrics by Fred
Ebb; Based on the play *Chicago* by Maurine Dallas Watkins; Directed
and Choreographed by Bob Fosse; Settings by Tony Walton; Costumes
by Patricia Zipprodt; Lighting by Jules Fisher.
*Cast*: Gwen Verdon, Chita Rivera, Jerry Orbach, Barney Martin.

This was the mythical stage musical depicted in the movie *All That
Jazz*. When Bob Fosse was compelled to have a heart bypass and postponed directing *Chicago*, Paddy Chayefsky, Herb Gardner, and I were
regular visitors at New York Hospital where the operation was to be
performed. Fosse asked Chayefsky to read his will and when Paddy discovered he wasn't mentioned; he screamed at Fosse to live. I also recall
the day of the operation, Gwen Verdon called and told me that Bob had
left me $10,000 to throw a wild party in the event he died. I told Gwen
to tell him I would do it for $5,000. (She did, and Bobby laughed all the
way to the operating room.)

Fosse was weak from the ordeal, yet he returned to direct *Chicago* because he felt he owed it to Gwen. It was much too soon and I wasn't

surprised when, after a rocky opening in Philadelphia, he asked if I would help him fix the show; my billing was to be "Associate Friend." Fosse gave me 1% of his royalty (rising to 1½% on recoupment) and a major headache; I was trying to pull together all the insecure passions of the authors, stars, and producers who felt they were being abandoned. Fortunately the original *Pippin* designers, musical and backstage staff, and former chorus members—all now involved in the creation of *Chicago*—stood in the path of their friendly fire, and urged me to help them save the show. There was so much that was brilliant in the musical: a great score, a unique form, a dynamite cast, and dance numbers to stop your heart; *Chicago* didn't need saving so much as it needed editing.

It must have been John Kander's experience as a dance arranger that inspired him to compose some of the best vamps in musical theatre history; "Willkommen" from *Cabaret*, *Zorba*'s "Life Is," and the seven quarter-notes followed by a dotted sixteenth-note pick-up made the vamp to "And All That Jazz" from *Chicago* the best. (It was so good that Marvin Hamlish wrote a variation on it for "One" from *A Chorus Line*.) Vamps are gateways to a song, insistent musical suspensions telling you something wonderful is coming. And Kander and Ebb didn't let us down with their brash 1920 Chicago-Dixieland-Creole-Jazz-Band opening number.

W. C. Fields's tombstone read: "Better here than in Philadelphia," and no wonder; trying out a musical in the city of brotherly love could be deadly business. "And All That Jazz" was staged on a rising elevator from the orchestra pit (the band was on stage), and one night the elevator fell from the stage level down the trap to the basement. Fortunately no one was hurt, but the show was canceled that evening. I'll never forget the next day's performance and the shaken but gallant Chita Rivera; rising in view on the repaired elevator, singing Ebb's masterful period reference lyrics and holding on to the newly installed hand railing for dear life!

Staged as a cynical vaudeville show (MC and all), each character had their stage turn. "Mister Cellophane" was written for a cuckolded husband, and as played by Barney Martin, Amos was the only character in the musical you really cared for. Fred Ebb and Fosse gave Martin the shambling stage persona of Bert Williams—top hat, shabby dress suit, very large shoes—and most significantly, with a wonderful Kander slow ragtime refrain, reinvented Williams' trademark song, "Nobody."

Chita Rivera said they called Bobby and me "Gloom and Doom" because of the cuts and new musical numbers I asked to be put into the show. Kander and Ebb wrote "When You're Good To Momma" under duress, since it required eliminating their favorite character, an agent (played by David Rounds), and the song "Mr. Ten Percent." Rounds wrote to thank me after being fired and landing the starring role (now legendary) in the musical *Herringbone*. It was difficult enough for Fosse having to fire an actor—he was always insecure of being fired himself—but putting "Nowadays" in as a new finale for Gwen and Chita was a heartscald.

We were in the musty downstairs Forrest Theatre bathroom lounge—the only other place to rehearse while the stage was being used—and Fred and John had just finished playing the new song. It was a sardonic duet, replacing a not-so-funny (nor musical) drum and saxophone bit by the two stars. Both ladies were delighted, but when we asked Gwen to start the song, she announced that "Nowadays" would be sung as a single, *by her*. The smell of fear filling the room was even stronger than the disinfectant smell of the men's room urinals, and a cue for Kander and Ebb to disappear. "This is mine, Fosse. No more for the good of the show. It's mine!" By now Chita was in tears, imploring me to give the number to Gwen, and Fosse was dazed. (He later told me he wanted to quit, then and there.) I quickly sat our dance arranger Peter Howard at the piano and asked him to play the song and ignore the hysterics. Peter began playing and Gwen, now also crying uncontrollably, yet not leaving, started the song! Chita, hearing her, came to the piano, and through her tears sang her part of the duet. During what seemed like an eternity, the tears stopped and the two stars sailed into the second chorus, now laughing and hugging each other. After it was over and all was forgiven and forgotten, except by me, I turned to Bobby and said: "I want 2%."

As it turned out, the show was a hit, and after a few months of receiving Fosse's promised royalties (our gentleman's agreement), he said I was rich enough and stopped paying me. "Everything about it is appealing. . . . " And all that jazz.

If Bob Fosse ever needed a theme song it would have been "Razzle Dazzle," because the dialogue he and Fred Ebb wrote for the character of the showbiz-lawyer, Billy Flynn, came straight from his crooked heart. Bobby told me he thought of himself as "a fraud with a couple of good dance steps." He was a genius, of course, and died much too soon, leaving a creative musical theatre legacy second only to Jerome Robbins. I once wrote a line for Bob Fosse in the movie *All That Jazz*, which he loved: "I always look for the worst in people, and usually find it." His tragedy was wanting to believe it.

Shubert Theatre
Opened Sunday, October 19, 1975
Joseph Papp presents a New York Shakespeare Festival Production in
association with Plum Productions:

# A Chorus Line

Conceived, Choreographed and Directed by Michael Bennett; Book by
James Kirkwood and Nicholas Dante (with some gratis jokes from Neil
Simon); Music by Marvin Hamlisch; Lyrics by Edward Kleban; Co-
Choreographed by Bob Avain; Settings by Robin Wagner; Costumes by
Theoni V. Aldredge; Lighting by Tharon Musser.
*Cast*: Donna McKechnie, Kelly Bishop, Pam Blair, Wayne Cilento, Pris-
cilla Lopez, Robert LuPone, Sammy Williams.

Ed Kleban worked for Columbia Records under Goddard Lieberson
during the golden days of Original Cast Recordings, learning all he could
from the Broadway musical theatre writers. I recall him submitting an
original musical, *Gallery*, and how imaginative the words and music were.
I agreed to produce it (Kleban's first musical with Peter Stone writing the
book), and was surprised when he told me the project had to be put on
hold while he collaborated with composer Marvin Hamlisch on another
musical, *A Chorus Line*, which was being "workshopped" at the Public
Theatre.

A *Chorus Line* was about eighteen dancers who were desperately auditioning for the chorus of a new musical; they revealed their innermost
hopes and frustrations with eternal showbiz pathos: "I need this job / Oh
God, I need this show." Hamlisch and Kleban's score was a seamless
joining of scene and song; it had good tunes, and included an especially
romantic waltz refrain, "At the Ballet." The dancers' stories were not so
far from their real life experiences. Listen to Cassie, a featured dancer
down on her luck (Donna McKechnie), pleading with her former lover
Zach, the director-choreographer (read Michael Bennett) in "The Music
and the Mirror": "All I ever wanted was the music, and the mirror, and
the chance to dance for you." The author's assignment to contrast each

character was humorously fulfilled with "Dance: Ten; Looks: Three," an esoteric reference to the dancer's "bod." Kleban's lyric is outrageous and Hamlisch is smart enough to get out of its way by setting the words in a bright tempo and lilting triplet figures to punctuate the jokes. "What I Did for Love" was the hit ballad I expected Hamlisch to write—sentimental and lush, the kind of song you hear under a movie's main title. When I first listened to it in 1974, it seemed ordinary compared to the quality of the rest of the score. Since then, the plague of AIDS has ravaged the ranks of Broadway singers, dancers, actors, choreographers, and directors—notably, Michael Bennett—and twenty years has proven the song not only to be tragically prophetic, but unbearably poignant: "Kiss today good-bye and point me t'ward tomorrow / We did what we had to do / Won't forget, can't regret what I did for love." A *Chorus Line* was the first landmark musical since *Hair* in 1968, and possibly the last of the twentieth century.

# 1976–1977

Alvin Theatre
Opened April 21, 1977
Mike Nichols presents:

## Annie

Book by Thomas Meehan; Based on "Little Orphan Annie" comic strip; Music by Charles Strouse; Lyrics by Martin Charnin; Musical Numbers Choreographed by Peter Gennaro; Directed by Martin Charnin; Settings by David Mitchell; Costumes by Theoni V. Aldredge; Lighting by Judy Rasmuson.
Cast: Andrea McArdle, Dorothy Loudon, Reid Shelton, Sandy, as "Arf."

Roger Stevens, the distinguished producer and progenitor of the Kennedy Center in Washington, D.C., and I were celebrating his commission of the architectural plan for the Musical Theatre Lab's new home on the Terrace Floor of the Center. Roger was also an investor in *The Apple Tree, 1776,* and *Pippin,* and was asking my advice about another musical, *Annie.* Its Broadway producers wanted to book the now coveted Kennedy Center, plus a $300,000 investment; they boasted that they had Mike Nichols set to direct Charnin and Strouse's original Goodspeed Opera House production. (I had seen the production the summer before in East Haddam; my daughter Julie was a techie on the working crew, and together with fellow techie Billy Berloni, she found Sandy, Orphan Annie's dog, at the local pound.) I thought *Annie* could be a big hit and urged Roger to invest, but not to replace Martin Charnin, who had nourished this project for years, as director. Roger, remembering *The Apple Tree*, agreed, and invited me to the premiere at the Eisenhower Theatre in the Kennedy Center.

Peter Gennaro's contribution to the staging of the numbers was inestimable, especially his work in keeping the treacle out of the child-orphan's scenes and his choreography of a raucous dance, "Easy Street," topping Dorothy Loudon's over-the-top performance. After the opening, I sent Strouse the following telegram: "I saw *Annie* in previews last week and I cried twice: Once when Annie sings "Maybe" and then again at the end of the show when the curtain came down and I realized I wasn't the producer." Charles Strouse does what good composers do; he constantly writes music. He can compose a tone poem for watching a raindrop as easily as writing "Maybe" for an orphan. His penchant for running the scale ("Put on a Happy Face") is apparent in the first four bars of this lovely ballad. With a simple B-flat triad, Strouse sets the essential tone of sincerity and saves this child's prayer for her birth parents from becoming a phony tearjerker. He follows the refrain with a bridge full of complicated accidentals (to further neutralize the lyric's sentimentality), but Strouse and Charnin press their luck with the last four bars. Setting "Tomorrow" in G-flat gave all the pubescent Orphan Annies a fighting chance to belt the octave and four range refrain: "Tomorrow, tomorrow, I love ya tomorrow, you're only a day away," and ruined more young voices than cigarette smoking. Whenever Anna in *The King and I* felt afraid, she held her head erect and whistled a happy tune. Stuck with a day that's gray and lonely, this Annie sticks out her chin and grins and says: "Oh the sun'll come out tomorrow." What a difference a day makes.

# 1977–1978

## *All That Jazz* (The Movie)

Bob Fosse and I were on a roll. *Pippin* and *Chicago* were established stage hits when Bob suggested we continue our partnership in the movies. He told me I'd love Hollywood, producing films and making certain he threw up before each take. (At the time I was writing my first play, *Stages*, encouraged by Stephen Sondheim, who generously acted as my dramaturge. The play was inspired by Elisabeth Kübler-Ross's *On Death and Dying*, and I still can remember the creative exhilaration of being more than "someone who knows a writer.") Sam Cohn, Fosse's canny agent, and Barry Diller, then head of Paramount Pictures, kept nipping at my heels to come up with an idea for Bob's next movie. I found a four-character book by Hilma Wolitzer entitled *Ending*, also about death and dying, which I thought would stretch Fosse to direct a string quartet, rather than a symphony orchestra of a film, and also would help me write my play. Both assumptions were wishful thinking.

I hired Robert Alan Arthur for $30,000 to write the screenplay and sold it to Diller with a budget of three million dollars. When we arrived on the Gower Paramount lot, Bob and I were given the Sam Spiegal–Elia Kazan bungalow, used by them during the filming of *The Last Tycoon*. Bob Fosse was the reason for Diller's green light, so naturally he took the larger (Spiegal) office, but I was thrilled at the thought of working in Kazan's space; he was a theatre giant I greatly admired. Screen stars paraded in daily, for cocktails and "chats," until I asked Bob when we were going to have them audition. Bob replied that they had been auditioning; we didn't have to hear them read the part because it was all in the eyes.

It suddenly dawned on me that I was in a la-la land that had nothing to do with my theatre experience or talent. It was all about being photogenic, and shooting enough film so that the director could create any performance he wanted, simply by editing. What was I doing here? The coup de théâtre happened the next day. As I drove into my parking space, the Paramount custodians were *stenciling my name, in yellow paint, over Gage Kazan's!* I couldn't breathe; I called Sam Cohn to tell him that I was leaving for New York that afternoon, and that Bob could have my share of the picture for any inconvenience I might have caused.

Immersing myself in completing *Stages* and self-producing it on Broadway (a grave miscalculation), with Richard Foreman directing, momentarily restored my equilibrium. Audiences for the thirteen sold-out previews were thrilled and I recall the casting director Scott Rudin telling me it was the best new play he had seen in years. On opening night, however, the Broadway establishment hated it, and I knew we had closed during the first act. Edward Albee said I should have used a nom de plume: "They would never let a producer think he could write." The kicker to this anecdote is that *Ending*, the intimate movie I commissioned about a young married man dying in a hospital, became *All That Jazz*, a musical extravaganza about Fosse's heart attack. Bob's film career stayed alive by his dying on screen; my writing career died by trying to stay alive on stage.

# 1978–1979

Uris Theatre

Opened Thursday, March 1, 1979

Richard Barr, Charles Woodward, Robert Fryer, Mary Lea Johnson, and Martin Richards, in association with Dean and Judy Manos present:

## Sweeney Todd, The Demon Barber of Fleet Street

Music and Lyrics by Stephen Sondheim; Book by Hugh Wheeler; Based on a version of "Sweeney Todd" by Christopher Bond; Directed by Harold Prince; Dance and Movement by Larry Fuller; Production Design by Eugene Lee; Costumes by Franne Lee; Lighting by Ken Billington; Orchestrations by Jonathan Tunick.

Cast: Angela Lansbury, Len Cariou, Edmund Lyndeck, Victor Garber.

(To open the Uris Theatre in 1974, Jimmy Nederlander booked a terrible musical entitled *Up*, directed by Peter Hall. It wasn't until someone pointed out that "Up-Uris" wasn't the most fortunate marquee coupling that they changed the name of the show to *Via Galactica*.)

*Sweeney Todd* was a heavy scenery show; to save the cost of moving it from an out-of-town tryout to Broadway, the producers decided to preview it for four weeks in the cavernous Uris (now called the Gershwin) Theatre. The decision nearly sunk this remarkable musical, but nevertheless failed to warn future shows of the perils of in-town tryouts. There is a perverse underground of Broadway wise guys, jealous professional competitors, and media gossipmongers who delight in being the first to watch a new creation struggle to perfect its imperfections. These search-and-destroy predators spread the word that *Sweeney Todd* was in trouble, and it took the supreme confidence of its creators to ignore the audience walk-outs during early previews. Their steadfast belief was finally realized in the last few days before opening, and it resulted in a triumph.

*Annie*, which ran for 2,377 performances, was the quintessential children-family musical, and Stephen Sondheim's revenge was to write *Sweeney Todd*, a grisly dread Broadway musical for grown-ups. "The Ballad of Sweeney Todd," a foreboding Greek Chorus prologue, sets the tone of the evening: "He shaved the faces of gentlemen / Who never thereafter were heard of again." Then as if to emphasize the gravity of the message, the Chorus intones three endings to the musical sequence. "Johanna," a love song, not cited often enough as part of Sondheim's oeuvre, is also a favorite audition piece for tenors. (I hear it each time I produce a musical and usually hire the actor singing it.) It has uncommon beauty and surprise, and although we've listened to 150 years of "Jeanie with the Light Brown Hair," I still feel Johanna. The theme of *Sweeney Todd* is revenge, and Len Cariou made you feel the sickening satisfaction of cutting your enemies' throats. "Pretty Women" was one of the most frighteningly beautiful scenes I ever saw. Angela Lansbury's memorable portrayal of a woman who grinds up murdered humans and sells them as meat pies remains disturbingly indigestible, and her cockney accented delivery of Sondheim's tricky lyrics was a miracle, as was her intonation. Hal Prince didn't stint with this production, and I loved how he filled the theatre space with organs and iron foundries. (There are some who thought a modest off-Broadway revival was superior to Prince's epic vision. Burp.)

This seminal work elevated past attempts (*Candide, The Most Happy Fella*) and bridged the gap between musical theatre and opera into a new form. *Sweeney Todd* was neither opera, operetta, musical drama, nor musical comedy, but a meld of all, creating a new American work of art. I recall the thrill of seeing the last preview and wish I was the one who sent Steve the opening night telegram that read: "Bake a Leg."

# 1979–1980

Broadway Theatre
Opened Tuesday, September 25, 1979
Robert Stigwood in association with David Land presents:

## *Evita*

Lyrics by Tim Rice; Music by Andrew Lloyd Webber; Directed by Harold Prince; Sets, Costumes, and Projections by Timothy O'Brien and Tazeena Firth; Lighting by David Hersey; Sound by Abe Jacob; Choreography by Larry Fuller.
*Cast*: Patti LuPone, Mandy Patinkin, Bob Gunton.

England's Andrew Lloyd Webber and Tim Rice landed on Broadway in 1971 with *Jesus Christ Superstar* and were tolerated by the colonists. *Evita*, however, was a full-scale invasion. It won all the Broadway awards (and deserved them), the London Album was on every national radio and television station, and you couldn't get a seat (even in the huge Broadway Theatre) for months. "The British are coming!" was the cry heard from the New York Times tower on 43rd Street to the Shubert Theatre's 44th Street atelier-office, and across the street in the Sardi Building, where Dramatists Guild members joined hands to pray for a second American revolution.

"Don't Cry for Me, Argentina" demonstrated Evita Peron's mesmeric hold on her public. She was a consummate politician who could turn adversity into advantage, who explained that her rise from poverty (and prostitution) to riches hadn't changed her: "The truth is I never left you / All through my wild days, my mad existence / I kept my promise / Don't keep your distance." The Rice-Webber score was thrilling, and it was matched by wonderful performances from LuPone and Patinkin, and by Harold Prince's fortunate repeat choice of *Sweeney Todd*'s Larry Fuller to make the show dance (especially in a stunning execution of Fascist marches by military uniformed Peronisters). Everything about *Evita* was revolutionary: subject, score, staging, sets, casting, financing, and most of all, the British Crown on American musical turf.

# PART IV
## 1980–1990

# Less Is Less: *Cats*, *Les Misérables*, and *The Phantom of the Opera*

Broadway produced only three new hit musicals in five seasons, from 1976 to 1981, compared to four new hit musicals (in one season) in 1950. We were bankrupt. What were we doing about replenishing the treasury of American musicals? I tried my best by restoring the endangered purpose of the Musical Theatre Lab, moving it from the Kennedy Center to Harvard-Radcliffe, and from commercial management (my fault, I fear) back to artistic experimentation.

Together with composer Robert Waldman, bookwriter Conn Fleming, and lyricist Alfred Uhry (who in a few years would write *Driving Miss Daisy*), I produced and directed the musical *Swing*. Robin Wagner's floating bandstand (powered by compressed air) literally lifted a twenty-piece dance band off the ground and turned it 360 degrees. It was spectacular, as was designer Richard Pilbrow's introduction of fiber optics to theatre lighting, in order to create a constellation of stars for the finale, "Dream Time." The show almost worked during its Kennedy Center tryout. William Safire wrote some gratis jokes (one about Harold Ickies—his name got a laugh), Pat Birch came to fix some numbers, Jerry Bock came to hold my hand, but Janet Eilber (a Martha Graham alumna) and Debbie Shapiro didn't need any help from anyone to light up the stage with their "Good from Any Angle" and "Michigan Bound." It wasn't their fault the show closed. It was the director, stupid. On Broadway, Norman Lear and I presented *The Moony Shapiro Songbook*, introducing the very talented Jeff Goldblum, whose performance nearly tore the roof off the Morosco Theatre six months earlier than its actual demolition. The regional theatre expansion was inevitable, given the Broadway malaise, but their limited stage space and financial resources provided little opportunity for increasingly expensive new musicals. Michael Bennett's *Dreamgirls* caused a stir, but mostly revivals of past Broadway hits filled the vacuum until the arrival of the phenomenon, *Cats*, in 1982.

This decade was to be dominated by three imported British musicals and the talents of two English showmen: Andrew Lloyd Webber and Cameron Mackintosh. Mackintosh produced *Cats*, *The Phantom of the Opera*, and *Les Misérables*. (Rule, Britannia! Britannia, rule the waves!) He introduced the limited advance booking methods of the West End—permitting a few months advance ticket sales to a hit show in order to keep the ticket tight—and raised the level of theatre advertising to new heights. These three shows revolutionized Broadway theatregoing and cloned international companies of themselves, creating an aura of celebration regarding the original New York and London productions. Tourists from all over the world flocked to see the Broadway versions, and in the absence of exciting homegrown American musicals, the tri-state area of approximately 15 million people selected *Cats*, *Les Miz*, or *Phantom* as the one event they had to experience on their birthday, anniversary, honeymoon, prom night, etc. It became a new lifestyle rite of passage. Less was more.

The British musicals' extraordinary success continues after sixteen years; they occupy the best Broadway houses and have caused a backup of productions wanting to play New York. With the exception of Stephen Sondheim, American musical dramatists were stifled, and the Broadway landlords did little or nothing to bolster their hopes, being content with the prospect of having their flagship theatres filled into the millennium. Less is less.

# 1981–1982

Imperial Theatre
Opened Sunday, December 29, 1981
Michael Bennett, Bob Avain, Geffen Records, and The Shubert
Organization present:

## *Dreamgirls*

Book and Lyrics by Tom Eyen; Music by Henry Krieger; Directed and
Choreographed by Michael Bennett; Co-Choreographed by Michael Pe-
ters; Scenery by Robin Wagner; Costumes by Theoni V. Aldredge;
Lighting by Tharon Musser; Sound by Otts Munderloh.
*Cast*: Sheryl Lee Ralph, Clevant Derricks, Jennifer Holliday, Loretta
Devine, Ben Harney.

The best thing I did for *Dreamgirls* was to drop a number from *Swing*
("The Love Jitters") featuring Sheryl Lee Ralph, and to release her contract just in time for her to land in Michael Bennett's workshop and play
one of The Stepp Sisters (a.k.a. The Supremes). The direction and choreography (Michael Peters of Michael Jackson "Thriller" MTV fame) for
this Motown musical was as original as Robin Wagner's three dancing
light towers that revolved to give each locale a different look throughout
the evening. Jennifer Holliday was a handful, on- and offstage, but her
rendition of "And I'm Telling You I'm Not Going" was as exciting as a
Pentecostal church meeting, so everyone put up with her behavior. The

balance of the score served the staging of the show more than the characters' innermost desires and frustrations. Rather than hearing a song that made me "feel a thought," Eyen and Krieger's songs made me notice a light cue. Their theme of corruption in the music business resonated in the big cities, but outside of Detroit, New York, Los Angeles, and a few other cities, *Dreamgirls* was just too hip. Possibly, another problem hindering the spread of this musical was the lack of trained black singer-dancer-actors throughout the country to mount local professional or amateur productions.

# 1982–1983

Winter Garden

Opened Thursday, October 7, 1982

Cameron Mackintosh, The Really Useful Group, David Geffen, and The Shubert Organization present:

## Cats

Based on *Old Possum's Book of Practical Cats* by T. S. Eliot; Music by Andrew Lloyd Webber; Directed by Trevor Nunn; Associate Director/Choreographer, Gillian Lynne; Design by John Napier; Lighting by David Hersey.

*Cast*: Betty Buckley, Ken Page, Harry Groener, Terrence V. Mann.

When my partner Norman Lear told me there was a new hit musical in London called *Cats*, and that we should bring it to Broadway, my first thought was, oh no, not a show about Joel Grey's father! At the time we were producing *American Passion*, an original musical by Fred Burch and Willie Fong Young about the media corruption of children's dreams, which presented a wonderful cast for their off-Broadway debuts: Robert Downey, Jr., Todd Graff, Laura Dean, Jane Krakowski, and Martha Plimpton. *American Passion* ran for forty-three performances; *Cats* will run for forty-three years. The potency of the Webber-Nunn hit song, "Memory," established the aura surrounding this unusual musical concerning felines—not to be confused with Katz. The song is Andrew Lloyd Webber at his best: a soaring melody, complicated rhythmic cadences within the first eight bars of the refrain, and a modulation to lift the last chorus to the heavens.

Belting D-flats above the scale was an effortless task for chest-singers the likes of Betty Buckley, Elaine Paige, and Patti LuPone, but the thought of hitting a D-flat sent every theatre soprano into despair as they vainly tried to disguise the break in their voices. The great opera composers—Verdi, Puccini, Mozart—cast sopranos as leads; then in operetta and musical theatre (except for Merman) they followed the practice. Composers wrote for the voice with a range from middle C, upwards for two octaves. A trend toward casting untrained singers (comediennes, dancers) as musical theatre leads began in the fifties and sixties and reached its zenith with Barbra Streisand in *Funny Girl*, whose voice could reach a remarkable emotional climax without resorting to head tones. She inspired contemporary composers such as Coleman, Kander, Hamlisch, Strouse, and Webber to write for the more modern, emotional belt range. It's fitting, twenty years later, that Streisand's recording is what made "Memory" such a hit.

The show's sets and lighting heralded the return to *The Black Crook*–type musical extravaganzas of the late nineteenth century: spectacular scenic effects, flamboyant costumes, a ballet company, and a quite negligible plot. The *Cats* setting was a great garbage heap with trap doors for tomcats, pussycats, tabbycats, and chessycats to enter and exit with ease. (One critic said it made him feel like something was peeing on his leg for two hours.) The musical also featured a deus ex machina finale that delivered Betty Buckley's Grizabella into cat heaven. John Napier and David Hersey repeated the device (with a helicopter) for *Miss Saigon*. Broadway was now into theme park entertainment, following Michael Eisner's Disney dictum that *business* is the operative word in the phrase show business.

For Andrew Lloyd Webber, it was a stunning solo breakaway from partner Tim Rice and caused the establishment of The Really Useful Group; his production firm later became a cash cow. *Cats* has grossed over a billion dollars, and RUG was sold to a recording/publishing conglomerate for millions more in profit. The logo-slogan, "Now and Forever," on the *Cats* poster proved to be prophetic.

# 1983–1984

Ethel Barrymore Theatre

Opened Sunday, December 4, 1983

James B. Freydberg and Ivan Bloch, Kenneth-John Productions, and
Suzanne J. Schwartz in association with Manuscript Productions
present:

## *Baby*

Book by Sybille Pearson; Music by David Shire; Lyrics by Richard
Maltby, Jr.; Musical Staging by Wayne Cilento; Scenery by John Lee
Beatty; Costumes by Jennifer von Mayrhauser; Lighting by Pat Collins;
Film Design by John Pieplow.
*Cast*: Liz Callaway, Todd Graff, Martin Vidnovic, Catherine Cox.

David Shire and Richard Maltby, Jr., should have been the next new
kids on the block; they had paid their off-Broadway dues with *Starting
Here, Starting Now*. Then, however, they explored separate careers; Shire
moved to scoring motion pictures in Hollywood and Maltby became the
puzzle maven for *New York Magazine*—following Sondheim's example to
the extent of using the same agent and living across the lane in Roxbury.
But their love of theatre never wavered and *Baby* proved to be a touching
and mature musical about the pain and passion of giving birth.

Liz Callaway and Todd Graff's performance of "What Could Be Better"
was utterly charming, and "I Want It All" was a funny, liberating

battle cry for the growing feminist movement. Shire wrote a beautiful melody for "The Story Goes On," which required the range of an Yma Sumac. He was fortunate to have Callaway to make it through eight shows a week. The song suited the author's ambitious explanation of the biological chain of evolution. Pointedly, there was no mention of the Supreme Being; however, with a rising emotional melodic line, thundering crescendo, and an ascending sixteenth-note arpeggio accompaniment, the number ends the act sounding a little like the voice of God.

Although *Baby* had a short run, a measure of the musical's value is the high demand for stock and amateur performances, especially on the college campus. (My favorite Lizzie was Kate Ostrow, at the University of Michigan, in a delightful production without the unnecessary film intrusions of the Broadway version.) Maltby and Shire's next musical was to open thirteen years after *Baby*. Continuity has all but disappeared for musical dramatists. *The Pajama Game, Damn Yankees, Fiorello!*, and *Tenderloin* were written in consecutive seasons. Writers from the fifties to the seventies seldom had to wait more than a year or two before presenting their next musical. Today they may have to wait five years before they can play their refrain. Too long to vamp.

---

Booth Theatre

Opened Wednesday May 2, 1984

The Shubert Organization and Emanual Azenberg by arrangement with Playwrights Horizons present:

## Sunday in the Park with George

Music and Lyrics by Stephen Sondheim; Book by James Lapine; Directed by Mr. Lapine; Scenery by Tony Straiges; Costumes by Patricia Zipprodt and Ann Hould-Ward; Set and Costume Designs adapted from the George Seurat painting *Sunday Afternoon on the Island of The Grand Jatte*; Lighting by Richard Nelson.
*Cast*: Mandy Patinkin, Bernadette Peters.

Impressed with James Lapine's *Twelve Dreams*, Steve Sondheim teamed up with him and Playwrights Horizons to experiment with *Sunday in the Park with George*. It was an inspired collaboration: a new generation bookwriter-director, designer, and producer working with the most challenging musical dramatist of the day. I was thrilled with the first act of the musical and bewildered by the second. No matter, it won all the awards and reclaimed the American musical high ground.

Mandy Patinkin was once again passionate and intense, and could hit high notes only a nightingale would recognize. His "Finishing the Hat" was the personification of work-obsessed George Seurat. Bernadette Peters had acquired a grace I'd not noticed before, doubtless due to Sondheim's music and lyrics—or it might have been that stiff, Seurat-bustled costume—whatever, she was divine. Lapine and Straiges's stunning evocation of the famous Seurat painting, "A Sunday Afternoon on the Island of La Grande Jatte," was a theatrical thrill.

"Move On," written in five sharps, gave piano accompanists fits, but once under their fingers the beauty of the song overwhelms the exercise. Nearly three octaves, the melody climaxes, breathes, then climaxes again, keeping you constantly involved—no, inspired—by its lyric: "Anything you do, let it come from you / Then it will be new"; this is precisely what Sondheim continues to do, continues to be. When Frank Loesser died, Steve and I were working on *The Girls Upstairs*, and he told me how sad it felt "not having anyone to hit the ball back over the net." Sondheim is still playing tennis by himself.

# 1986–1987

Broadway Theatre
Opened Thursday, March 12, 1987
Cameron Mackintosh in association with the JFK Center for the
Performing Arts (Roger L. Stevens, Chairman) presents:

## Les Misérables

Music by Claude-Michel Schonberg; Lyrics by Herbert Kretzmer; Original French Text by Alain Boubil and Jean-Marc Natel; Additional Material by James Fenton; Based on novel by Victor Hugo; Directed and Adapted by Trevor Nunn and John Caird; Designed by John Napier; Lighting by David Hersey; Costumes by Andreane Neofitou.
Cast: Colin Wilkinson, Terrance Mann, Randy Graff, Francis Ruffelle.

"Do You Hear the People Sing" from *Les Misérables* is a stirring anthem for revolt at the barricades; it is rendered by a huge chorus waving red flags on a set that seems to undulate with each refrain. "On My Own," a song of unrequited love, has a tender melody and some originality in a heartfelt but mostly derivative musical score.

The original London production of *Les Miz* (title truncated by *Variety*) was produced in association with the prestigious Royal Shakespeare Company. How Cameron Mackintosh persuaded the heavily subsidized RSC to mount a commercial production with British taxpayers' pounds is a secret marvel of entrepreneurial acumen. He was to repeat the same feat

with the Royal National Theatre with his production of *Carousel*. It's no
wonder they knighted Mackintosh; he has financed nearly as much theatre as the British Arts Council. Much to his credit, he envisioned this
passionate musical from hearing a French recording and seeing a concert
performance of Schonberg and Boubil's score. The songs throbbed with
Pigalle-milieu-Edith Piaf-type angst, of hopeless love and intense suffering. With English translation help from a former newspaper critic, the
French authors musicalized almost every moment of Victor Hugo's masterpiece and social chronicle. The result was an uncharacteristically long
musical—the story of a criminal, Jean Valjean, who serves as an example
of the misery and contradictions of society. Nunn and Caird repeated
their *Nicholas Nickleby*, RSC-styled adaptation of a classic novel, and this
Common Market collaboration couldn't have arrived at a more propitious
time, to quench the thirst for a smash hit after a three-year drought of
Broadway musical theatre.

# 1987–1988

Majestic Theatre
Opened Tuesday, January 26, 1988
Cameron Mackintosh and The Really Useful Company present:

## The Phantom of the Opera

Music by Andrew Lloyd Webber; Lyrics by Charles Hart; Additional Lyrics by Richard Stilgoe; Book by Richard Stilgoe and Andrew Lloyd Webber; Directed by Harold Prince; Musical Staging and Choreography by Gillian Lynne; Production Design by Maria Bjornson; Lighting by Andrew Bridge.
*Cast:* Michael Crawford, Sarah Brightman, Steve Barton, Judy Kaye.

When I saw *The Phantom of the Opera* at Her Majesty's Theatre in London, 1987, there were long lines of ticket buyers patiently waiting to buy any returned seats for the day's performance. Something extraordinary was happening. (The phenomenon continues today, in New York and London.) Andrew Lloyd Webber had produced, composed, orchestrated, written the book, and cast his wife as the lead in a penny-dreadful story of a deformed genius composer who haunts the Paris Opera House and mesmerizes the leading lady. *Beauty and the Beast* meets *Trilby*.

"The Music of the Night," as performed by Michael Crawford, captured the creepy madness of the Phantom, and the audience couldn't wait to see what was hidden behind his chic half-face mask. The mask became the logo/trademark for *Phantom*, and Cameron Mackintosh repeated his marketing success (like the *Cats* cat's eyes, and the urchin of *Les Miz*). Erudite critics wrote of the musical's falling chandelier as a symptom of the meretricious style of its creators, but Webber and Company understood their audience all too well. The hit song and the production shared an excess of melodrama, and in less musically experienced hands could have been laughable. Webber's penchant for meditating on phrases of familiar themes, yet being wholly original, is his great strength and mettlesome critique. Beginning in D-flat, he states the leitmotiv, adding an extra 2/4 bar to complete the refrain. Then comes a surprising change of key for the first three bars of the bridge. He repeats the chorus and bridge twice before ending with the hypnotic leitmotiv a third time: "Let the dream begin, let your darker side give in to the power of the music that I write / The power of the music of the night." Kitsch? Perhaps, but never underestimate the madness of the crowd.

---

Eugene O'Neill Theatre
Opened Sunday, March 20, 1988
Stuart Ostrow and David Geffen present:

# M. Butterfly

By David Henry Hwang; Directed by John Dexter; Scenery and Costumes by Eiko Ishioka; Lighting by Andy Phillips; Music by Giacomo Puccini; Additional Music by Lucia Hwong; Peking Opera Consultants, Jamie H. J. Guan and Michele Ehlers.
*Cast:* John Lithgow, B. D. Wong, John Getz, Rose Gregorio, George N. Martin.

In 1986, Hal Prince and I were working on a crossover musical based on Andre Malraux's *La Condition Humaine* (*Man's Fate*) with composer Philip Glass and playwright David Henry Hwang, when Prince received Andrew Lloyd Webber's offer to direct *The Phantom of the Opera*. Alarmed Prince would shelve our musical before I could get everyone under contract, I rushed to Paris, hired an avocat, and stormed the publisher Gallimard's office in hopes of obtaining the rights to the deceased author's novel. With an introduction from Prince, I managed to meet with Malraux's daughter, Florence (film-maker Alan Renais' wife and co-executrix of her father's estate), who told me she was in favor of our adapting the novel, but the power to decide was Gallimard's. (What she didn't say was that her husband didn't care for Glass' music.) After several meetings in Paris, it was clear that Gallimard was not about to license their French demigod's masterpiece to a Chinese American and three New York Jews. In addition to their anti-Semitic and anti-American bias, French intellectuals think Broadway musical theatre is akin to the Folies-Bergere.

Everything happens for the best. Prince went on to direct *Phantom*, and Hwang sent me a two-page proposal for a musical about a *New York Times* story of a French diplomat who had fallen in love with a Chinese actress who subsequently turned out to be not only a spy, but a man. In his Afterword of the published play, David said: "I remember going so far as to speculate that it could be some 'great, *Madame Butterfly*–like tragedy'. Stuart was very intrigued, and encouraged me with some early funding." When David finished M. *Butterfly*, it was a play with Puccini's music—not the musical I thought I had commissioned. But after reading the text, I knew immediately I had to produce it on Broadway, with John Dexter as the director.

John Dexter was forever sending me books. He was the best informed man on the arts (all of them) that I ever knew, and his direction of M. *Butterfly* required that I be as well prepared as he. The enemy was pretentiousness. Dawdling actors were told to get on with it, designers were ordered to make the costume or set change work better, and when he met with a disgruntled CEO representing my co-producer, who said, "change the script or I'll eat you up," John replied, "I'm indigestible." Indeed. I often wonder, if there was a musical around at the time that excited me as much, would I have taken on this straight play? Suffice it to say, I imagined M. *Butterfly* as a musical on an epic scale, off the ground, and I produced it accordingly. I could never discover rigid method or policy in producing activities. It seemed to me that continually shooting arrows into the air—hoping that they might fall somewhere that counted—was a good thing. The idea is to be all over the place, poking your nose in everywhere, nipping at the heels of the creators, always prodding, like a very small shepherd dog, pushing them relentlessly to some pasture that you had decided would be good for them. Not that all the artists I've encountered have been sheep. During the M. *Butterfly* tryout at the National Theatre in Washington, I said to David Henry Hwang, "I wish you would write a speech about deception." Coming out of a clear blue sky, the suggestion shocked David. He said, "What do you mean, Stuart?" "Oh, I don't know," I said. "Just a speech about delusion . . . deception." I've forgotten what David said, but I was certain he thought it was one of the silliest and vaguest ideas he had ever heard. Now the strange fact is that, two days later, he wrote a speech for the French diplomat who thought his lover was a Chinese opera diva: "I'm a man who loved a woman created by a man," the duped diplomat said, "to feel the curve of her face, the softness of her cheek, her hair against the back of my hand," and then confessed, "I knew all the time somewhere that my happiness was temporary, my love a deception; but my mind kept the knowledge at bay, to make the wait bearable." There it was—a speech about deception! An arrow shot in the air. As for the business end of producing, I don't know how to tell a young man or woman what to do in order to acquire the enthusiasm and haphazard hope necessary to be a kind of small Hercules, where no Augean stable is too big to clean if one has to clean it to get a show on. This story may help.

My first face-to-face meeting with David Geffen was for lunch, at Barbetta, on West 46th Street. It was some six months after the M. *Butterfly* Broadway opening and a few weeks since we had won the Tony Award for Best Play of the 1987–1988 season. It had been a tough, long journey—braving the storm in David Henry Hwang's skiff made of paper—and a triumph for those who refused to keep their dreams within reason. Not so, however, for Geffen. He was my General Partner, but had not yet seen one performance of the celebrated production. Now, ten months later, we were enemies suing each other for substantial violations of our Joint Venture Agreement, and the fancy fish Geffen had ordered for lunch wasn't going down with the white wine.

When I first asked him to read the play, to my delight, he responded by putting up a million dollars of the $1.5 million budget. What excited me more than the investment was the promise that Geffen and I would work together. Michael Bennett had told me Geffen was helpful promoting *Dreamgirls*, and I assumed his reputation as a hip record/music man would enhance the marketing of my risky play. *Not.* I knew something was seriously wrong with the decision when Geffen didn't show up in Washington for the National Theatre tryout, but sent his CEO instead—a Rolex-watched lawyer, with no theatre experience. I was momentarily relieved when, after seeing two preview performances, the Rolex praised our work and flew off into the Western sunset. Then came the devastating Washington reviews; but they were not as threatening as the return of the Rolex, accompanied by his New York, Paul Weiss firm attorney. They demanded that we take out all the political references, all that "Brechtian bullshit" about Mao and the Revolution, and said that if we refused, Geffen wouldn't give us a cent to bring it into New York. Clearly, they had abandoned their belief in the metaphor of East and West that David had written, and threatened Sunset Boulevard blackmail if we didn't accede to their prurient interests. I told David Hwang and John Dexter that we were in bed with tyrants and the trick was not to get screwed. Box office business was terrible, but the writing and acting was being focused by a genius director, and the play was ultimately realized. I went to the bank to mortgage our Pound Ridge home, and loaned the Partnership $472,000 to get us to Broadway. Three months, seven Tony nominations, four Outer Critics Circle Awards, and one injunction later, M. Butterfly was the toast of the town and David Geffen was furious. Tyrants may forgive you for being wrong, but they'll never forgive you for being right.

He was fashionably late for our lunch, and wore a white T-shirt and jeans. Our conversation was pointless, and the check came to $136.76. Geffen didn't carry a wallet, so I used my credit card and gave him $20 cash for the tip. He smiled, and told me not to worry, I'd get the money back (I did, by messenger that afternoon), and as the aisle of waiters parted for him, he added that he thought M. Butterfly would be a paragraph in his biography.

# PART V
## 1990–1998

## Stomp, Rent, Bring in 'Da Noise Bring in 'Da Funk: Quo Vadis?

The nineties continued the recycling of mainstays of the Broadway canon: *Gypsy*, *The Most Happy Fella*, *Guys and Dolls*, *Man of La Mancha*, *She Loves Me*, *Camelot*, *My Fair Lady*, *Show Boat*, *Carousel*, *Hello Dolly*, *Damn Yankees*, *Grease*, *The King and I*, *How To Succeed in Business Without Really Trying*, *A Funny Thing Happened on the Way To the Forum*, *Annie*, *Candide*, *Chicago*, and a vanity production of the off-Broadway *Once Upon a Mattress*.

The first sign that something new was stirring came from England in 1994; it was an event entitled *Stomp*. Featuring a performance art group that uses everything but conventional percussion to make rhythm and dance, *Stomp* generated a different kind of musical theatre energy and was the precursor to the 1995 *Bring in 'Da Noise Bring in 'Da Funk*. Savion Glover was a force of nature and a tap-hammer witness to the painful, shameful, African-American experience that was made curiously entertaining by the Public Theatre. *Rent*, by Jonathan Larson, also opened in 1995, and shows every sign of becoming a landmark musical. Tragically, the author died before opening night and we'll never know how much further he might have taken us out of the Broadway wasteland, or how many new artists he could have inspired to write the next landmark musical. Until then, I'll take *Rent* five hundred twenty five thousand six hundred minutes at a time.

Notwithstanding the sinking of the original *Titanic* ocean liner, the 1996–1997 Broadway season brought two new musical survivors to the surface: *Titanic*, book by Peter Stone, music and lyrics by Maury Yeston; and *Jekyll & Hyde*, by Frank Wildhorn and Leslie Bricusse. The former was conceived, written, and practically produced by Stone, whose penchant for imagining hit musicals connected with historical events (*1776*) paid off again, due in part to lackluster competition, but mostly because of the inspired direction by Richard Jones, who mythologized the voyage. Jones had the actors on a three-tier set, representing the various passenger classes onboard; they addressed the audience as if it was the ocean itself. Possibly in an effort to exonerate the audience's complicity, after hitting the iceberg and foundering, the *Titanic* creators resurrected the cast for a sentimental epilogue. Yeston's scholarly score is not necessarily for the common man but "There She Is" was a fanfare to begin the evening worthy of Aaron Copland.

The second survivor was the critically battered *Jekyll & Hyde*, a showboat with a hull made of plastic—the CD recording of its score, released a year in advance of the Broadway opening. The power of a hit recording—especially the playing of "This Is the Moment" for television ice-skating competitions—had audiences transformed even before witnessing Doctor Jekyll turn into Hyde on stage. Thankfully, Frank Wildhorn's popular melodies overwhelmed Leslie Bricusse's lyrics, but unfortunately, Robert Louis Stevenson's romantic adventure and fantasy was lowered to a threepenny musical pulp production.

The verisimilitude of African folk songs and pop music was artfully realized with the score to *The Lion King*, a unique musical that inaugurated the 1997–1998 Broadway season. "Circle of Life," "Can You Feel the Love Tonight," "He Lives in You," "One by One," "Shadowland," and "Endless Night," by Elton John, Tim Rice, Lebo M, Hans Zimmer, Mark Mancina, Jay Rifkin, and Julie Taymor, are all evidence of the extraordinary collaboration. The Disney team got it right this time by hiring avant garde director Julie Taymor to create a live theatre event, and not a duplication of their successful animated film. It was an inspired (and gutsy) choice. Taymor's experimental theatre background, from Japanese Bunraku to staging Wagner opera, and her knowledge of puppets and masks, inspired her to create onstage characters that were both animal and human. Look for Disney, now a major player as both landlord and producer, to purchase the Shubert Foundation, and the air rights above all their Broadway theatres, in order to produce more live theatre based on their films, and to transmaglorify Times Square into the ultimate international theme park.

*Ragtime* was to have been producer Garth Drabinsky's apotheosis. Having organized a Canadian corporation, Livent, Inc., with public funds (possibly from Saskatchewan fur trappers) and the profits from his Toronto production of *The Phantom of the Opera*, he worked a Ponzi-type scheme in which belief in the nonexistent financial success of *Kiss of the Spider Woman, Candide*, and road companies of *Show Boat* was to cause investors to pay for future productions. It nearly worked. The vaudeville played out by Drabinsky and a willing press was as entertaining as "The Crime of the Century" written by Stephen Flaherty and Lynn Ahrens for the Evelyn Nesbit character to sing in *Ragtime*. However, like General Patton, Drabinsky moved far ahead of his supply line and ran out of gas. As for the musical—Graciela Daniele, Eugene Lee, Santo Loquasto, and Jules Fisher made Frank Galati look like a director, and I thought the writing was shamelessly sentimental, pandering to the worst clichés regarding Jews and African Americans. A safe, sanitized version of America's profound struggle with democracy, imagined by a Canadian hustler. One of Broadway's more colorful part-time producers (his real job was breaking legs), after reading his show's unanimously bad opening night reviews, said: "That's the last time I do a play with an author." I was reminded of his hubris when I read the notices for *Fosse*—the latest milking of the cash-cow-choreographer's past.

I first played poker with Bob Fosse when he was married to Mary-Ann Niles. He had the same gimmicks then, and could bluff you with a pair of deuces. Dressed in black, from his socks to pork-pie hat, smoking a dangling Camel cigarette, he'd give you that baby-face deadpan stare so you weren't sure if he was going to slug you or kiss you if you dared call his hand. He played the same game with me after we did *Pippin* and *Chicago*; he asked if I would produce a musical adaptation of the Italian film *Big Deal on Madonna Street*. Fosse had held the stage rights for years, and buoyed by the success of *Dancin'*, he wanted to repeat the use of old standards for the score; he was tired of staging mediocre songs in order to make the writers look good so they could make more money than he did. I disagreed, and convinced him to let me option Peter Allen, Craig Carnelia, and several other promising new songwriters to write a score to order. Indeed, Peter wrote a terrific song for *Big Deal* called "Ain't I Something," and I bet on it bringing Bobby to the table. It didn't; Fosse folded and went to another producer, leaving me with a full house but no pot.

Perhaps the "lack of soul" critics allude to regarding Livent's *Fosse* has everything to do with the hauteur of its producer. What a perfect hand: no conflict, character or catharsis to dramatize, no writers to collaborate with, no story to tell! It's a sure thing.

# 1990–1991

Eugene O'Neill Theatre
Opened Sunday, February 10, 1991
Stuart Ostrow and Andrew Lloyd Webber present:

## La Bête

By David Hirson; Directed by Richard Jones; Sets and Costumes by
Richard Hudson; Lighting by Jennifer Tipton.
*Cast*: Tom McGowan, Michael Cumpsty, Dylan Baker, John Michael
Higgins, James Greene.

*La Bête* came to me in the mail, in rhymed couplets. I was astonished
by its form and language and intrigued at the chutzpah of its author, David
Hirson, in assuming that any commercial producer would produce a
seventeenth-century comedy of manners. Of course, the perversity of de-
viating from correct Broadway fare has always attracted me, and Hirson's
gift for creating a timeless satiric commentary and a penetrating explo-
ration of eternal human foibles compelled me to go forward. There was
something else: a sense of unique theatrical scale, a feeling of being in a
tilted world, off the ground, which as I discovered with M. *Butterfly* was
akin to producing musicals. Furthermore, both Davids, Hwang and Hirson, were first-time Broadway playwrights, and I was convinced there was
an audience for risky theatre. When, after many meetings, I learned David
was Roger (*Pippin*) Hirson's son, I was certain the Gods were with us.

What I didn't figure on was Ron Silver and the new search-and-destroy policy of the *New York Times*.

Just as I knew when I read M. *Butterfly* I wanted John Dexter to direct, Richard Jones and Richard Hudson were my first choices to direct and design *La Bête*. (I had seen their production of *Too Clever By Half* in London.) Andrew Lloyd Webber joined me as co-producer, and casting the leading role of Valere was our priority. Meg Simon assembled a brilliant company and suggested Robin Williams for Valere, but after his bad experience with the Mike Nichols/Lincoln Center production of *Waiting for Godot*, he passed. It was at my instigation that we went to London to audition Ron Silver for the lead, and although Richard, Meg, and David had qualms about Silver, I believed that the conman quality he had conveyed successfully in films and recently in David Mamet's *Speed-the-Plow* (for which he won a Tony) would complement the absurdity of the part, as well as Valere's potential for mischief and harm. Wrong.

When Silver came to me during the last week of rehearsals after a disastrous run-through (he had not yet learned his lines) and asked if I would like to replace him, I attributed it to the usual actor jitters before a first public performance, and encouraged him to open in Boston as scheduled. After ten days of technical rehearsals in Boston, his agent Sam Cohn called to say Silver still wasn't ready and asked me to postpone the opening. It was then I came to the realization that Silver would never perform regardless of how many hi-ho's I entreated. He missed several previews and on opening night his understudy, Tom McGowan, went on and received rave notices. That caught his attention, and Silver finally performed the following evening. He was so unsure of his lines he had arranged a code with an off-stage prompter to cue him if he recited the following couplet: "I do not want to disappoint the house, so let me get my next line from John Kraus." When Richard and David heard Ron utter this horrific ad-lib on stage they went into cardiac arrest, and I decided to replace him. Silver and I agreed that the announcement would attribute his leaving to "artistic differences," and that neither of us would talk to the press. Silver, however, had a field day, publicly accusing Jones of directing him to play the character gay, and suggesting I influenced the favorable *Boston Globe* review for the play and for McGowan (as if anyone could influence the late "Killer" Kevin Kelly).

The New York gossip media had changed the rules of the game. In the past, you went out-of-town to prepare the show for the New York critics, and you didn't advertise any good local reviews. In return, the Broadway press wouldn't write about the show until it was ready—after it came to

New York—and you lived or died on what was written opening night. We never did overcome the damage from all the controversial media attention, and despite the Tony nominations and awards for writing, design, direction, acting, etc., *La Bête* closed after fifteen previews and twenty-four performances on Broadway. When *The Independent* in London called asking for my comment on the occasion of *La Bête* winning the 1993 Olivier Award for Best Comedy, I replied, "If I win any more awards for *La Bête*, I'll be totally bankrupted."

# Afterword

Producing theatre today is very expensive—partnerships, even with the devil, are necessary—and I have made a few bargains with the Angel of Death. Although I've thought at times, "The fornication I'm getting isn't worth the fornication I'm getting," at least my partner's checks didn't bounce. Now that I'm producing the new musical drama *Doll* by Michael Korie and Scott Frankel, to be directed by Robert Wilson in Vienna in 2000, prior to Broadway, I am determined not to have my finger pricked again. However, I do smell the brimstone.

To be present at the creation of an original musical is what interests me most; helping to fuse subject, story, and song into a completely new theatrical metaphor is a unique assignment, and it is of little interest to the current crop of Broadway wise guys. They are only end-game players. Even though the gestation period is normal, the delivery of a new Broadway musical can take anywhere up to five years. This means one must advance pre-production expense for everything, including options, fees, workshops, transportation, casting, legal, and accounting (sometimes as much as $250,000, which is what *Doll* has cost to date) before there is a dollar of investment capital or box office income.

*Doll* is based on factual events. Set in 1914 Vienna in the months leading up to World War I, it is the true story of the scandalous love affair between Gustav Mahler's 35-year-old widow, Alma Schindler Mahler, and the younger Expressionist painter, Oskar Kokoschka; when Alma breaks off their affair to become another man's muse, Kokoschka has a life-size doll created as her fully functional surrogate. It's a cinch.

When Scott Frankel and Michael Korie asked me to produce their musical drama about a man who has carnal knowledge of a life-size doll,

I thought, "Oh, my God, another dive off a tall building into a sponge." And I said yes. I admired Scott as a composer (remembering his exciting music from an otherwise negligible project), and Michael Korie's lyrics were the best I had heard since Sondheim's. Obsession is the theme of the show; it is the story of one man's ecstasy of illusion over reality, set against the backdrop of the dying Austro-Hungarian Empire. It is provocative and dangerous—essential stimulants for an equally moribund Broadway.

While planning Act One of *Doll*, I was also beginning Act Three of my life. Having accepted Dr. Sidney Berger's and the University of Houston's offer to be the Cynthia Woods Mitchell Distinguished Professor of Theatre Chair (including a laboratory for my new musicals in return for joining Edward Albee and Jose Quintero as a member of the School of Theatre faculty), I now had a venue for *Doll* and for the dormant Musical Theatre Lab. Given the media's penchant for disaster gossip concerning new productions, the University was also a safe place in which to experiment.

In 1973, I had had the eleemosynary impulse to originate a Musical Theatre Lab and I contributed $250,000 for the purpose of creating new musical theatre works. When I told my lawyers and accountants that the Stuart Ostrow Foundation, Inc., would have no proprietary rights in the works created they were incredulous, and the theatre world was quick to co-opt the MTL process for commercial gain. As a result, the credo of every non-profit organization today aspiring to "create musical theatre" is in reality, "how much can we make from it?" Since I galvanized the monster, it's only fitting that I should attempt to restore its soul. When the SOFoundation negotiated the first "workshop" agreement with Actors Equity Association and originated the Musical Theatre Lab at St. Clements Church, our premiere musical was *The Robber Bridegroom* by Robert Waldman and Alfred Uhry, starring Raul Julia. (It went on to another life with John Housman's Acting Company, starring Kevin Kline and Patti LuPone, and as a Broadway production with Barry Bostwick.) Much has been attributed to the workshop process originated at St. Clements, developed at the Kennedy Center, Harvard, and now productive at the University of Houston. The SOF Board of Directors was the best and brightest: Ingram Ash, Jerry Bock, Edgar Bronfman, Schuyler Chapin, Bob Fosse, Goddard Lieberson, William Safire, and Stephen Sondheim.

The Musical Theatre Lab produced twenty-six experimental musicals, some distinguished, all dedicated to creators seeing how far they could take their work, as opposed to seeing how much they could make from it. It was a place where Maurice Sendak, the famous artist, and Carole

King, the pop songwriter, created *Really Rosie*, and playwright Arthur Miller wrote lyrics for Stanley Silverman's music for *Up from Paradise*. The MTL also gave the first American commission to Robert Wilson, to produce a musical work based on *Medea*.

These "gypsy run-throughs" were rehearsed with Actors Equity Association members (at a sixth of weekly union scale salary) for four weeks, and performed five times over an additional two-week period, with six days of rewriting time after the second performance. No reviews were permitted. They were performed with no scenery, no lighting, in rehearsal cloths, with makeshift props, and were accompanied by one piano. This was done for several reasons—to emphasize improving the material more than presenting a finished production, and to allow no limitations as to size of cast and style of production.

When Michael Bennett came to St. Clements, he thought he was in heaven. The realization of rehearsing and performing a new musical inexpensively was just what he had needed in order to implement his concept of a musical about Broadway gypsy-dancers. He went to the nonprofit Public Theatre, and together with Joe Papp, applied to Equity for the MTLab formula and mounted *A Chorus Line*. Rehearsing for a year at bargain basement prices, Michael recorded the ambitions, secrets and disappointments of various Broadway gypsies (many from *Pippin*) until he had a text and score. The results were stunning, and this was one of the great rip-offs of the actor's union, which prompted the landlord of the Sam S. Shubert Theatre (where *A Chorus Line* transferred) to say, "There's no profit like non-profit."

*Doll* inaugurated the reincarnated Musical Theatre Lab at the UH School of Theatre. Professional actors and students were cast to interpret the musical and all went well until the initial reading. After listening to the first act of the score, played by Scott, and the text, read by the cast, our New York professional director excused herself, telling me she was feeling quite ill. She was never to return. Given the emergency, I postponed rehearsals and reluctantly informed the cast I would replace her as director. The New York City Opera actress cast to play Alma Mahler was understandably distressed at her departure and tried to convince me to hire an opera director to rewrite the musical so that she could play both Alma and the surrogate doll created by Alma's obsessed lover. The suggestion was the very antithesis of the author's intention and was as shocking as her allusion to the departed director's agreement with her interpretation. Thankfully, Suzan Hanson flew in from Los Angeles to replace the diva and the attempt to hijack *Doll* was averted.

The workshop was a success. It shifted the theme of the musical from fanaticism to obsession, and the protagonist in the text from Alma Mahler to Oskar Kokoschka. New songs for Oskar were written, and the finale of the musical was dramatically altered. The task of finding a director who could take *Doll* to a higher level by creating a world to match its unique theatricality was daunting. Many celebrated directors were approached, with varying results. The English and German artists were thrilled with the material, but not available for years, while the American directors thought the sex and violent events in the musical were too lurid and too risky for Broadway. I sent the score and book to Robert Wilson, who, sixteen years after our Musical Theatre Lab's *Medea*, was now the preeminent postmodernist. He loved *Doll* and agreed to direct it. Cast thy bread upon the waters.

Gallows courage? Perhaps. *1776, M. Butterfly, La Bête*, and *Pippin* were all tough sells, yet they made theatre history. Happily, there is an angel in the wings who has put up the first million dollars for *Doll*, and we have begun our journey to Broadway. What saves me from the slough of despond and keeps me going? Curiosity. Will I surrender to the dark side, or will next year find me less concerned and the theatre world more composed? With luck and another five million dollars, I should have the answer.

# Bibliography

Aleichem, Sholom. *Tevye and Other Stories*. Moscow: Schocken Books, 1987; Ruduga Publishers, 1988.

Banham, Martin. *The Cambridge Guide to Theatre*. New York: Cambridge University Press, 1992.

Benet, Stephen V. *The Devil and Daniel Webster*. New York: Gallahad Books, 1994.

Bergman, Ingmar. *Smiles of a Summer Night*. New York: Simon and Schuster, 1960.

Bissell, Richard. *7 ½ Cents*. Boston: Little, Brown, 1953.

Bond, Christopher. *Sweeney Todd*. New York: Samuel French, 1974.

Carruth, Gorton. *The Encyclopedia of American Facts and Dates*. Thomas Y. Crowell, 1972.

Dennis, Patrick. *Auntie Mame*. Chicago: Harcourt and Brace, 1958.

Dennis, Patrick. *Little Me*. New York: Dutton, 1961.

Dickens, Charles. *Oliver Twist*. London: Oxford University Press, 1949.

Edwards, Sherman, and Peter Stone. *1776*. New York: Viking Press, 1970.

Eliot, T. S. *Old Possum's Book of Practical Cats*. New York: Harcourt Brace Jovanovich, 1982.

Feiffer, Jules. *Passionella*. New York: Random House, 1982.

Fellini, Federico. *Nights of Cabiria*. Secaucus, N.J.: Citadel Press, 1985.

Gallico, Paul. *The Seven Souls of Clement O'Rielly*. New York: Doubleday, 1963.

Gammond, Peter. *The Oxford Companion to Popular Music*. New York: Oxford University Press, 1993.

Garraty, John A., and Jerome L. Sternstein. *Encyclopedia of American Biography*. New York: Harper & Row, 1974.

Gay, John. *The Beggar's Opera*. Lincoln: University of Nebraska Press, 1969.

Gottfried, Martin. *Broadway Musicals*. New York: Harry N. Abrams, 1980.

Howard, Sidney. *They Knew What They Wanted*. New York: Doubleday, Page & Company, 1925.

Hugo, Victor. *Les Miserables*. London: Fawcett, 1961.

Hwang, David Henry. *M. Butterfly*. New York: Penguin Books, 1989.

Jablonski, Edward. *The Encyclopedia of American Music*. New York: Doubleday, 1981.

Landen, Margaret. *Anna and the King of Siam*. New York: John Day Company, 1944.

Laszlo, Miklos, and Joe Masteroff. *the Shop Around the Corner—She Loves Me*. New York: Dodd, Mead, 1963.

Lederer, Charles, and Edward Knoblock. *Kismet*. New York: Random House, 1954.

Lee, Gypsy Rose. *Memoirs of Gypsy Rose Lee*. New York: Harper, 1957.

Lengyel, Melchior. *Ninotchka*. New York: Dramatists Play Service, 1961.

Lerner, Alan Jay. *My Fair Lady*. Coward McCann, 1957.

Leroux, Gaston. *The Phantom of the Opera*. Oxford: Iris/Clio, 1988.

*Little Orphan Annie*. New York: Dover Publications, 1933.

Matlaw, Myron. *Modern World Drama: An Encyclopedia*. New York: E. P. Dutton & Co., 1972.

McKenney, Ruth. *My Sister Eileen*. New York: Harcourt, Brace & Company, 1938.

Mead, Shepherd. *How To Succeed in Business Without Really Trying*. New York: Simon and Schuster, 1959.

Plaut, W. Gunther. *The Torah: A Modern Commentary*. New York: The Union of American Hebrew Congregations, 1981.

Plautus. *The Plays of Plautus*. New York: Macmillan, 1985.

Runyon, Damon. *The Idyll of Sarah Brown*. New York: Penguin Books, 1992.

Shakespeare, William. *Romeo and Juliet*. New York: Cambridge University Press, 1992.

Shaw, Bernard. *Pygmalion*. London: Penguin Books, 1974.

Smith, Betty. *A Tree Grows in Brooklyn*. New York: Harper and Row, 1947.

Stockton, Frank. *The Lady or the Tiger?* New York: Gallahad Books, 1994.

*Theatre World*. 41 editions. Editors: Daniel Blum (1950–1964); John Willis (1964–1990). New York: Greenburg, 1950–1957; Philadelphia: Chilton, 1957–1964; New York: Crown Publishers, 1964–1990; New York: Applause Theatre Books Publishers, 1991.

Thorlby, Anthony. *The Penguin Companion to European Literature*. Harmondsworth, U.K.: Penguin Books Ltd., 1969.

Trapp, Maria Augusta. *The Trapp Family Singers*. New York: Lippincott, 1949.

Twain, Mark. *The Diary of Adam and Eve*. New York: Doubleday, 1957.

Updike, John. Testimony before a house committee considering a bill calling for a White House conference on the humanities. Reprinted in *The National Review*, 1980.

Voltaire. *Candide*. Paris: Bordas, 1975.

Wallop, Douglas. *The Year the Yankees Lost the Pennant*. New York: Norton, 1964.

Watkins, Maurine Dallas. *Chicago*. New York: Knopf, 1928.

White, T. H. *The Once and Future King*. Putnam, New York: 1958.

Wilder, Billy, and I. L. Diamond. *The Apartment*. New York: Praeger, 1971.

Wilder, Thornton. *The Matchmaker*. New York: Samuel French, 1985.

Willson, Meredith. *But He Doesn't Know the Territory*. New York: G. P. Putnam's Sons, 1957.

# Index

Adolph Green and Jule Styne. © Renewed. Stratford Music Corporation, Owner of Publication and Allied Rights throughout the World, Chappell & Co., Administrator. All Rights Reserved. Used by Permission. Warner Bros. Publications U.S. Inc., Miami, FL 33014.

"The Rain in Spain," by Alan Jay Lerner & Frederick Loewe. © 1956 (Renewed) Alan Jay Lerner (ASCAP) & Frederick Loewe (ASCAP). Chappell & Co. owner of Publication and Allied Rights throughout the World. All Rights Reserved. Used by Permission. Warner Bros. Publications U.S. Inc., Miami, FL 33014.

"Rose's Turn," by Stephen Sondheim and Jule Styne. © 1960 (Renewed) Norbeth Productions, Inc. and Stephen Sondheim. All Rights Administered by Chappell & Co. All Rights Reserved. Used by Permission. Warner Bros. Publications U.S. Inc., Miami, FL 33014.

"Show Me," by Alan Jay Lerner & Frederick Loewe. © 1956 (Renewed) Alan Jay Lerner (ASCAP) & Frederick Loewe (ASCAP). Chappell & Co. owner of Publication and Allied Rights throughout the World. All Rights Reserved. Used by Permission. Warner Bros. Publications U.S. Inc., Miami, FL 33014.

"Small World," by Stephen Sondheim and Jule Styne. © 1959 (Renewed) Norbeth Productions, Inc. and Stephen Sondheim. All Rights Administered by Chappell & Co. All Rights Reserved. Used by Permission. Warner Bros. Publications U.S. Inc., Miami, FL 33014.

"Some People," by Stephen Sondheim and Jule Styne. © 1959 (Renewed) Norbeth Productions, Inc. and Stephen Sondheim. All Rights Administered by Chappell & Co. All Rights Reserved. Used by Permission. Warner Bros. Publications U.S. Inc., Miami, FL 33014.

"Soon It's Gonna Rain," by Tom Jones and Harvey Schmidt. © 1960 (Renewed) Tom Jones and Harvey Schmidt. Chappell & Co. owner of Publication and Allied Rights throughout the World. All Rights Reserved. Used by Permission. Warner Bros. Publications U.S. Inc., Miami, FL 33014.

"There's Gotta Be Something Better Than This," by Cy Coleman and Dorothy Fields. © 1965 (Renewed) Notable Music Co., Inc., and Lida Enterprises, Inc. All Rights Administered by WB Music Corp. All Rights Reserved. Used by Permission. Warner Bros. Publications U.S. Inc., Miami, FL 33014.

"They Call the Wind Maria," by Alan Jay Lerner and Frederick Loewe. © 1951 (Renewed) Alan Jay Lerner and Frederick Loewe. Chappell & Co. Publisher and Owner of Allied Rights throughout the World. All Rights Reserved. Used by Permission. Warner Bros. Publications U.S. Inc., Miami, FL 33014.

"Try To Remember," by Tom Jones and Harvey Schmidt. © 1960 (Renewed) Tom Jones and Harvey Schmidt. Chappell & Co. owner of Publication and Allied Rights throughout the World. All Rights Reserved. Used by Permission. Warner Bros. Publications U.S. Inc., Miami, FL 33014.

"Wouldn't It Be Loverly," by Alan Jay Lerner & Frederick Loewe. © 1956 (Renewed) Alan Jay Lerner (ASCAP) & Frederick Loewe (ASCAP). Chappell & Co. owner of Publication and Allied Rights throughout the World. All Rights Reserved. Used by Permission. Warner Bros. Publications U.S. Inc., Miami, FL 33014.

"You'll Never Get Away from Me," by Stephen Sondheim and Jule Styne. © 1959 (Re-

## About the Author

STUART OSTROW is the Cynthia Woods Mitchell Distinguished Professor of Theatre at the University of Houston. His many award-winning Broadway and West-End productions include M. *Butterfly*, *Pippin*, and *1776*. He has also produced *La Bête* and *The Apple Tree*, directed *Here's Love*, was associate director of *Chicago*, and authored *Stages*.